Build Your Own Playground!

JEREMY JOAN HEWES

Photographs by Suzanne Arms

Drawings by Susan Colton

Build Your Own Playground!

A Sourcebook of Play Sculptures,

Designs, and Concepts from the Work of JAY BECKWITH

A SAN FRANCISCO BOOK COMPANY/HOUGHTON MIFFLIN BOOK

Houghton Mifflin Company   Boston   1974

Some of the photographs by Suzanne Arms have appeared previously in the *Pacific Sun*.

Additional photograph credits:
Karen Becker, p. 131; Thomas Chiosso, p. 211; Community Design Center, p. 98; Danielle Diffloth, pp. 56, 148, 150, 202 (right), 203 (right); Donna Emerson, dedication page (left), pp. 11 (top), 66 (right); Charles Frazier, pp. 4, 5, 19, 20, 39, 42, 47, 51, 67, 73, 119, 164, 181, 184 (left), 186, 187, 188 (top), 189 (bottom), 213 (right); Jeremy Joan Hewes, dedication page (top), pp. 13, 17 (left), 40, 62 (right), 121 (left), 127 (right), 133; Drew Langsner, pp. 143, 205 (bottom); Ben Spicer, pp. 99, 100.

Library of Congress Cataloging
in Publication Data

Hewes, Jeremy Joan.
 Build your own playground!

 "A San Francisco Book Company/Houghton Mifflin book."
 Bibliography: p.
 1. Playgrounds. 2. Beckwith, Jay.
GV423.H46   790'.068   74–11206
ISBN 0–913374–15–6
ISBN 0–913374–16–4 (pbk.)
ISBN 0-395–19894–1
ISBN 0–395–19966–2 (pbk.)

This SAN FRANCISCO BOOK COMPANY/HOUGHTON MIFFLIN BOOK originated in San Francisco and was produced and published jointly. Distribution is by Houghton Mifflin Company, 2 Park Street, Boston, Massachusetts 02107

Book design by Anita Walker Scott

To the child in us all

Contents

Foreword

For me, this book is like creating a playground; it makes concrete something that was only a vision. When you're building a playground, once you have a basic structure, you can say, "Aha! Here is our beginning. We can change it, we can add to it, we can make it bigger or smaller." Helping to put my playground-building experience into book form has been like making that basic structure, a source of information that could serve as a standard—not 100 per cent complete, or absolute, but a document that would give people a place to start.

Basically, this book is a hypothesis for an ideal world, or an ideal playground, or an ideal process of community action. And this hypothesis needs to be tested. Please give us the benefit of your doubt; check our figures, test our theories, let us know what you've added or changed to make the information more useful to you. My hope is that by building from the soil of many communities' experience, we can improve the standards by which environments are created for children.

It may be hard to believe that making beautiful places for kids to play is an important thing to do in this era, when not only civilization but mankind itself is threatened with extinction. Beauty may not feed the multitude but it nourishes the soul, and even with full bellies we will not survive if our spirit dies. When moms and dads, friends and neighbors, old folks and kids all come out to build together, a special magic is created that washes away any question about the importance of play and playgrounds. After only a few days' experience, people start feeling that they can do anything, and that feeling could literally change the world.

JAY BECKWITH
People at Play
P.O. Box 14173, San Francisco, Ca. 94114

Author's Note

My work with Jay Beckwith began three years ago when I joined a group he had organized to build play environments for animals at the San Francisco Zoo. Although I had intended only to gather material for a series of articles about alternative forms of community action, the lure of the idea, the people, and the animals was strong, and I went back many Sunday mornings to be among them. Since then, Jay and I have collaborated on several projects in much the same way that we have put together this book—discussing ideas, looking at pictures, asking questions until the subject began to take shape. Although most of the words are mine, the principal source for those words has been the informal, conversational presentations that Jay makes to community groups. *Some brief portions of his presentations are included in the first three chapters of the book, set off from the text by italics.*

Jay and I have worked together to chronicle much of his experience and design ideas, but it's important to remember that each of the playgrounds pictured here is unique to its own community, the parents and children who planned and built it. The reflections of some of the community people in this playground-creation process are included as captions for the photos between Chapters 2 and 3.

As an observer and a participant in this process, I have tried to convey both the specific planning and building information and a sense of what a community-built playground means to its creators. For Jay and for me, this book is an expression of the philosophy of positive community change that we share. It is our hope that the ideas and instructions here will help many people become observers and participants in creating play spaces for children everywhere.

JEREMY JOAN HEWES
San Francisco
April 1974

R. Buckminster Fuller

I think that playgrounds should be renamed "research environments." This is what the children are doing so vigorously. They are not playing. They are finding out how the universe works. This is spontaneous research which is inherently gratifying, often joyously gratifying. How wonderful to find out how to use gravity as an accelerator or a brake. Nobody is around to tell you or to give you the name gravity, but you learn quickly that the greater the drop, the more it hurts your legs. That is what Galileo's work with falling bodies was all about. You want to understand that invisible power that is working around for you; you wish to check out your theory on a slide.

Children learn about tension. They have got to tear a great many things apart to find something that won't tear, that they can spontaneously grab for to arrest the falling and anticipate leg shock or break. They don't have to know the names tension, compression, gravity, or acceleration, but they have to get very familiar with such phenomena before a sound emanating from somebody's mouth can develop a word meaning experience. City-born and -matured children have almost no access to operative research environments as have had the billions of humans in the millions of years of their occupancy on planet Earth's pre-city eons.

Playgrounds provide children with experience-fortified gratification of physical research. Thus, their intuitive assumptions of "can do" are proven; they are thereafter confident of their own capabilities for sensing and employing the principles operative in nature, such as gravity, flotation, wind resistance, tension, and compression. Teen-agers and adults then may successfully deploy into wilderness for such activities as mountain skiing, surfboarding, cross-country motorcycling, and flying kites.

Build Your Own Playground!

1 What Do Kids Need?

Playgrounds themselves are really nothing other than places that have been set aside for children. They're not safe; they're not special; they're really just the marked areas that it's okay to be in. Anyplace else you're going to get hassled: "Hey, kid, don't hang around the store. Go get someplace that you belong." Well, the only place a kid belongs is the playground.

Everyone pretty much agrees that kids need a place to play and that it shouldn't be the street or the sidewalk. But often that's as far as the agreement goes. School authorities don't want to leave schoolyards open after hours or on weekends, city officials don't want the grass and trees in their parks ruined, and landlords don't want their gardens trampled. Even if there is a playground in the neighborhood, odds are it's the kind of impersonal, barren place that some government paved over and forgot about.

In a growing number of communities, though, that situation is changing. Many people are no longer willing to leave all of the decisions and responsibility to the bureaucrats, but they are beginning to decide for themselves, among other things, what the neighborhood park or schoolyard will be like.

This initiative is one of the roots of the community-built playground.

In many places, too, creation of an environment for play is both an economic and a legal necessity. Most states require nursery schools to provide an outdoor play space, yet most of these facilities have such small budgets that purchase and installation of commercial play equipment is out of the question. In fact, because of their somewhat underprivileged status, co-op nursery schools have long been the basic proving ground for do-it-yourself playgrounds.

More recently, the impetus for community action has broadened, and saving money is now only one of several reasons for a group's decision to control a part of its environment. Another strong motivation is the desire of many people in the community to "do something for the children." A park or playground can be the focus of this energy, which otherwise might remain a worthwhile but undirected sentiment.

Why a Community-Built Playground?

Community control, economic need, and concern for children are all clear justifications for creating a neighborhood playground, and they also help make a case for the people's building it themselves. If we follow the logic that kids are going to play and that they should have a place of their own to do it, then it becomes a matter of defining "their own." One thing this means is that children should help make the decisions about their space. They have a right to see their visions reflected in the environment, but they probably won't get a chance if the work is left to the bureaucrats.

It makes a great deal of sense for the people who will be using the playground to have a major part in its creation; indeed, that's the only way they can get precisely the environment they want. A contractor or city construction crew isn't going to stand around while a group decides where to put the fire pole, for example; hired builders work from detailed plans and are seldom inclined to be flexible. The community workers, on the other hand, can afford to be easygoing. They can start with a pile of lumber and a vacant lot, making up their design as they go along and finding places for the trees or tires that people bring as the playground develops organically.

Probably the most important reason for the people of a community to fashion their own play spaces, however, is the investment their work represents. The value of the playground to both children and adults increases in proportion to their involvement in its creation. And the playground improves the common space of a community because it reflects the unique personality of the people who live there and it is tangible evidence of their belief in themselves.

We're really talking about environmental awareness, taking probably the most vital, active element of a community in terms of energy—the people with young children—and getting some environmental awareness into their heads. You can't talk to those people about changing city streets and downtown malls and things like that until they've had their hands in it.

One fact that is becoming increasingly clear is that "progress" doesn't necessarily mean an improvement in the quality of life. Our society is wrestling with that notion, trying to sort out the beneficial from the harmful, the necessary from the superfluous. This examination has led many people to the conclusion that, so far as change is concerned, the process is as important as the product.

The environment in general and playgrounds in particular offer a good illustration of this process-product equation. Children can be the barometer for the quality of environmental change, since kids get a message wherever they are. They're happy in an environment that says yes to them, a place that has been made with their help and where they can choose the games and make the rules. And if a place is phony, if no one cares about them there, they know it right away.

In short, the attitude with which a place has been planned and built rubs off. A locked gate to the city-built schoolyard, for example, tells kids they are not welcome there. Cans of paint, brushes, and an empty wall, on the other hand, invite children to leave their mark on the school. In both instances the message is clear and the kids respond in kind,

perhaps vaulting the fence and breaking windows, perhaps making the wall come alive with their ideas.

In addition, a community's taking charge of the process of environmental change often yields much more than a playground. When a diverse group of people works together for the children's fun, a special chemistry is created, and this spirit stays with the playground long after the hammers are silent. Then there are the skills people have learned and shared, the involvement of these parents in their neighborhood school or park, and the collective experience of creating a structure while, at least in a small way, improving the community's quality of life.

So much for inspiration. There are still a lot of problems to solve between wanting to do something for the kids and creating a process of environmental change. And of course those problems are somewhat different in each community. The important thing is that many groups have chosen to tackle the problems, and they are getting plenty of assistance.

One man who helps community groups create environments for play is artist and designer Jay Beckwith. He is one of the pioneers of community-built playgrounds, having made his living this way for five years. Beckwith, who likes to describe his work as play sculpture, has been involved in the creation of more than fifty playgrounds in California.

The community-built playground that Beckwith and other designers are helping groups plan and build is not the familiar

swing set, slide, and monkey bars made of steel, though each of those activities may be incorporated into the play space. Community-built playgrounds, which are usually made of wood, are large frameworks of interconnected platforms, ramps, tunnels, bridges, ladders, and much more. These wooden structures have a kind of rugged grace, a solid, handmade quality that is somehow reminiscent of a backyard tree house or a fort in a hollowed-out stump.

Although no two community-built playgrounds are alike, they do share some common features and objectives. Most groups are planning a play environment for large numbers of children and so must make the best possible use of their space. In addition, because the structures are built almost entirely by volunteer, unskilled labor, they have to be fairly easy to construct. These playgrounds also are designed to encourage "free play," that is, child-initiated activity that doesn't require adult supervision, since the community group usually wants a place that is always open to kids.

Jay Beckwith summarizes the community's design goals, as well as his own objectives, as the creation of child-centered spaces. In working with groups of parents and educators, he emphasizes the importance of recognizing children's needs and providing an environment that stimulates and supports them.

Safety

WHAT ABOUT SPLINTERS? The first time Jay meets with a group he gives a slide show that illustrates a variety of community-built structures, as well as many of his ideas about play. Early in the presentation someone usually asks, "But what about splinters?" The question is as real as splinters are, but it often suggests a great deal more—a rather startled response to seeing so much wood in a playground, parents' apprehension at the idea of their kids on apparatus such as they've never seen before, or perhaps just general skepticism.

One way to answer the question, and perhaps also to counter the skepticism or apprehension, is to turn it around. Beckwith may ask the parents if any of them have ever sat in the bleachers at a football game, or if they considered staying home because there might be splinters in the wooden seats. This brings the question back to the people's realm of experience and often can foster a more receptive attitude toward new ideas and information.

Practically, splinters have not been much of a problem in community-built playgrounds. In fact, contrary to expectations, the structures, which are sanded during construction, often become increasingly smooth from the constant polishing by kids' contact. On some playgrounds, they've even gone back and notched the wood so that children wouldn't slip off. So the answer to splinters, really, is to let kids play. In addition, careful inspection of the lumber's quality before purchasing, proper storage of the wood during construction, and application of a penetrating sealer will minimize its tendency to splinter.

RELATIVE SAFETY The question of splinters is a touchstone for another major concept, namely, that safety is relative and that there is no such thing as an absolutely "safe" playground. Because cars are one of the biggest killers of young children, for instance, safety must be considered in a broader context even when planning for kids' play. One way for a group to consider safety in relative terms is to ask, "As safe as what?" about the playground. Should it be as safe

for children as, say, riding in a car, or climbing around on a construction site, or taking a bath? A comparative look at the hazards of everyday activities and potential dangers on a playground usually broadens the group's view of safety.

This new perspective often comes from one of the community members. At one of Beckwith's early meetings with a school group, the concern for safety was especially strong, and after two hours of discussion the group had not agreed on any ideas for the playground. Finally one father stood up and said, "I don't care about all this safety stuff. My kid has to cross three streets to get to the playground, and nothing that can happen to him while he's playing is anywhere near as dangerous as crossing those streets." This kind of bluntly appropriate statement can serve as the catalyst a group needs to really get down to the job at hand, as it did for that father's community.

I think the most important thing we can do for the kids is trust them, trust them to take the chances that are appropriate to them, at the time when it's best for them. I kind of suspect that if you don't give a kid the chance to take a risk on a playground when he's five, he'll do it at a time which may be—in terms of society and in terms of the child himself—less appropriate. He's going to try something with a car when he's fifteen, or with a needle when he's twenty-one. What I'm trying to do is to make a place where kids can take chances at the time they choose to take the chances, not when society chooses.

RISK-TAKING Again, safety must be put in its proper perspective. To attempt to create an absolutely safe playground would contradict one of the principal characteristics of play, that it involves risks. Children are designed by nature to take chances; their bodies are resilient and able to take bumps and mend easily. Consider how many times a child falls down in the process of learning to walk; that same punishment would break bones in most adults' bodies.

Moreover, children have resilient bodies because they need to take risks in order to explore their physical selves and to find out what they can do. If this self-discovery is prevented, children are unable to recognize their own potentials. They won't develop confidence in themselves, for they won't know where their centers of gravity are, physically or psychologically. So the notion of safety must accommodate risk if the intimate environment—the psychological health of children—is not to be threatened.

RISK WITHOUT FAILURE Yet safety and risk need not be incompatible. It's possible to design for risk without failure, but the prerequisite is a thorough understanding of how children use the playground. The most basic fact is that kids will do everything. If it's possible, they're going to try it, so they need an environment where they can do everything.

Usually, too, the kids will be doing everything possible all at once. Jay Beckwith recalls that when he designed his first large playground, he studied the model and counted the number of different things the children

CHILD DEVELOPMENT

The way children develop and mature should be a fundamental consideration for anyone planning their environments. Particularly during the nursery and elementary school years, children are evolving personality structures that will affect the way they conduct all future relationships. Obviously a congenial environment that fosters social interaction is important to this progressive development.

The work of psychologist Erik Erikson has provided a basis for much contemporary child-development theory. Erikson's thinking is based on Freud and goes beyond that pioneering psychological work. The writings of Erikson, especially *Childhood and Society*, serve as standards against which new child-development studies are measured, and these very readable works provide a good stepping-off place for a comprehensive review of the psychology of children.

Basically, Erikson states that bodily functions and personality are inseparable in a child, and he demonstrates how the progressive discovery of "body modes" is linked to psychological development. As the child explores his body, the influences of the environment and the character of his experiences condition his style of relating to the world.

could do. He concluded that there were three hundred possible activities, which seemed to promise a fair amount of use for the playground before the kids would have tried everything. Beckwith went to that school on the first day the playground was to be used, and within five minutes he saw the kids do all three hundred possible activities, plus some he hadn't even thought of.

That kids will do everything is a consideration that many people who design play equipment or plan playgrounds overlook. They tend to think in terms of individual pieces of apparatus, which offer specific, and usually limited, experiences for children. The typical commercial swing set, for example, is well built, but it's made for only one activity—a child sitting down, swinging back and forth. If anything else happens on that equipment, such as two kids crowding into the same seat (probably standing up), a swinger trying to go sideways instead of back and forth, or somebody shinnying up the support poles while other children are swinging, disaster may result.

One way to lessen the chances for disaster on the playground is to provide versatile components that do not limit children to a single pattern of behavior. An alternative to the conventional swing, for instance, is a tire that is suspended on chains from a central bearing. Since the tire is held horizontally by chains at three places (rather than hanging vertically by one chain), several kids can climb on together; and since it hangs from one point, this swing can go in all directions. Safety is provided for by putting the swing well away from any obstacles, usually at the perimeter of a play structure, and by keeping the tire fairly close to the ground.

Another means of planning for nonfailure risk is to eliminate the "invisible" dangers, such as that of the traditional high, narrow slide. A young child gets in line for the slide automatically because everyone else does. But he may not know what he's getting into. When he gets to the top of the ladder and changes his mind because the slide is too steep, it's too bad because five kids are right behind him yelling for him to go down. And even if the ladder is clear, it's a lot harder to go down than up. The invisible dangers for this child are the lure into the unknown and the possibility that on such a high slide failure may be deadly.

This kind of slide can also be hazardous for the children who've mastered it, because for them it has the danger of boredom. A kid goes down the regular way three or four times and he's had it; it's not interesting anymore. So to keep it interesting, he begins to explore the risk potential of the slide. A child will go down on a bike, or one kid will ride down on another's shoulders, while a third runs up. The problem here is not simply that the children exceed the design limits of the slide, but that they are eight feet in the air when they do it. And too often, they're not on sand or dirt but on blacktop.

The alternative slide is low and wide so that kids can pass each other, go down together, and do anything they want. Nor does a child have to climb an eight-foot ladder to get there; this slide goes off a sizable platform, which the child can reach in several ways. A guardrail can also be put across the top of the slide so that a kid is less likely to fall or be pushed down the slide when she's not expecting it, and so that a child can't endanger herself and everyone else by riding a bicycle down it.

In addition to scaling down the risks of such components as swings and slides, the playground as a whole can likewise be planned for relative safety. Separating different types of activity is a first step in mapping out the play space; for instance, a nature area and its occupants won't last long next to the basketball court. Similarly, the components of an active-play center should be arranged so that children doing one thing will not run into some part of the structure or interfere with kids doing something else. Of course another way to avoid dangerous situations is to provide, if possible, all of the activities the children want; if the playground has a sandbox, for example, the kids are less likely to build their sand castles under a swing.

Ground cover is yet another means of planning for safety. Many school playgrounds are hard-surfaced expanses that were made to last the longest possible time with the least maintenance or attention; unfortunately, these blacktop or concrete areas also permit the least possible play activity. Soft material, such as sand or tanbark, is mandatory under an active-play structure, but a hard-surfaced playground doesn't preclude this. So long as adequate drainage is provided, the soft material can be spread on top of the hard surface wherever necessary, and a low retaining wall can easily be built to contain this added material. In fact, the

sand retainer in some community-built playgrounds is a low concrete wall designed and built by the children.

Play and Its Characteristics

Clearly such design solutions add to the safety of a community-built playground, but they serve other purposes as well. Once again, the slide is a good example. With the traditional slide, a child waits in line so that he can climb up and take a one-way trip, which is better described as entertainment than play. With the low, wide slide, however, the child has several choices of activity, so his behavior can be spontaneous, which is what play is all about.

The characteristics of children's play, such as spontaneous behavior, are as basic to playground design as planning for safety. What a community ideally is trying to create is an environment which is planned with the knowledge that kids will do everything and which offers both enjoyment and experiences that fulfill children's needs. And once it has come to grips with the notion that safety is relative, a group usually makes an easy transition to thinking about how play can happen in its space. In fact, there is often a moment at these community meetings when the room almost explodes with voices, each person eagerly offering his ideas for the playground or recalling some adventure from his childhood. When that happens the emphasis has shifted from apprehension or doubt to an open-ended consideration of play.

Play is supremely voluntary, and any behavior that is truly voluntary is the mark of an integrated person. I think the thing that we see in children as being unique is their intrinsic natural integration, which often breaks down as they become more and more complex people. The loss of childhood is really the loss of that kind of naive integration that is the condition of not knowing all the implications of life. Because many of us adults have lost touch with our childhood, we sometimes need to be reminded that play is acceptable behavior and that it's an important experience to foster in children. We needn't thrust them into being miniature adults at the age of seven.

Most of the characteristics associated with play can be placed in one of three general categories: social interaction, physical development, and learning. But certain other qualities defy such classification, yet are essential to any definition of play. These qualities include the voluntary nature of play, its spontaneity, and the integration of body, mind, and senses that is typical of someone playing.

SOCIAL INTERACTION   The social characteristics of play are probably the most conspicuous, especially since a community always must plan its play environment to accommodate lots of children. Moreover, the social aspects of play deserve consideration because community groups seldom have the resources to provide supervision for the playground at all times. So, in addition to planning for safety, a community often must create an environment that encourages unsupervised free play, as well as adult-directed activities.

The most basic social characteristic of play is that kids play with each other, no matter what the setting. This knowledge can be a source of relief to a community group with little money for play equipment, but it's also a challenge to devise a full range of choices and experiences for the children. One example of the alternatives to expensive apparatus is the tire swing, which is a simple and inexpensive source of fun for several kids at once. Beckwith usually suggests that a group plan at least one tire swing for the playground; in fact, he likes this alternative so much that he calls it "the incredibly social swing."

When children play together, they are developing ways of communicating with each other, a process that helps to form a basis for their behavior as adults. The individual qualities of play, such as imagination, are always enhanced by sharing. One child may think up a pretty elaborate situation, but it grows and changes when others join in. By allowing and participating in this augmentation of his imaginary world, the child is learning to handle the biggest challenge his environment can offer, that of another intelligence.

Play demands the segregation of a small group of kids because they're creating a world of make-believe. And if too many people get involved in the play, it suddenly stops working. I can convince four kids that I'm the archbishop, but forty kids I can't, 'cause somebody's going to say, "Well, I know the archbishop, and you ain't it." Or, "You're no spaceman—where's your helmet?" With three or four kids, you can do it.

Play likewise involves the creation of special communities, with secrets and rituals known only to the participants. These activities usually are limited to small groups (since it's not a secret if everybody knows it), and they require a certain degree of privacy. The notion of private spaces on the playground is often a bit unsettling to adults, but it needn't be. The children's reason for wanting to be away from the main flow of action is merely to create and sustain their imaginary world.

One social distinction that makes a playground valuable to children is the fact that the "normal" rules of behavior don't apply in that place. Kids can holler, touch each other, and be anybody they please out there. Quite often this freedom acts as a safety valve for children who resent the normal classroom routine or who simply can't cope well with school. For some children the playground may be the one place where they excel, thereby preserving their self-esteem and possibly saving them from social oblivion.

Clearly many of the social aspects of play are closely associated with the children's psychological climate. Fun is obviously healthy, especially when it's shared. Private games and fantasies also foster intimacy among children, offering a necessary foundation for future relationships. And in addition to helping alleviate some behavior problems, the freedom to have fun, to explore, and to take risks contributes significantly to the healthy growth of all children.

Humans are social animals, of course, and much of our play behavior can also be seen in other animal groups. Ethologists have attributed such aspects of play as spontaneity and the innate need to take risks to our animal nature and have done complex studies relating play to learning among the young of many species. Although these theories of play may not have specific application to playground planning, they are relevant to the process. By offering a new vantage point from which to view children's behavior, acknowledgment of our animal nature can add an instructive dimension to a group's percep-

ETHOLOGY OF PLAY

Ethology, the scientific study of animal behavior, bridges the gap between theories that attribute behavior primarily to heredity and those that claim that all learning comes from environmental experience. A principal ethological concept is that animals have innate tendencies to behave in certain ways, and the urge to play is one such inborn capacity in many species. This branch of science may be traced directly back to Darwin, but the father of modern ethology is the Austrian ethologist Konrad Lorenz, who is best known in this country for the book *On Aggression*.

The research methods developed by ethologists are quite valuable to the study of play in children, especially for persons who are interested in information that does not require the statistical procedures of psychology. Ethologists observe animals' natural behavior, create a model that explains how this behavior relates to survival of the species, and then test it through further observation and tests.

tion of play. And if nothing else, this body of knowledge serves as evidence that, like other young animals, children have both the instinctive need and the desire to play.

Beckwith always introduces the subject of animals' play in his discussion with a community group, usually by showing a slide of six or eight kids in a tree and likening them to their primate ancestors. Jay describes his work with a group of volunteers at the San Francisco Zoo observing animals and building play environments for them. Not only are there similarities between the animals' needs and those of children, particularly in the areas of muscle development and coordination, but the environment in which they must play is often the same too—concrete and steel. Of course the conditions for animals in zoo cages are more extreme than for children on a blacktop playground with a chain-link fence around it, but both environments must be improved to adequately support normal social development.

PHYSICAL DEVELOPMENT Play has traditionally been associated with children's physical development through sports and physical education. While these organized, often competitive activities are a useful part of growing, children can also benefit greatly from free play in stimulating surroundings.

Young children in particular need day-to-day physical experience to keep up with their changing bodies. A two-year-old, for instance, has learned to walk and probably can maintain a kind of shaky control over his movements, but his body has not yet reached its regular proportions. His head is big, his arms and legs short, his feet small, and his center of gravity high. Because those body proportions are changing continuously—the limbs growing larger in proportion to the head and the center of gravity moving downward—the child has to keep trying himself out to coordinate his actions and find his equilibrium.

A well-planned playground allows the growing child to determine her physical capabilities as she explores her environment. And anyone who has watched this process knows how carefully, and thus safely, a child goes about her exploration. Seeming to know

her limits, she'll climb to a certain point and no higher; when she reaches the edge of a stair or platform, she'll sit down and sort of slide to the level below. As she becomes more familiar with the environment and her muscles become accustomed to these new movements, the child will begin to move a bit faster and go a little higher. This process of exploring both herself and her environment keeps a child "centered" and gives her a sense of confidence and poise that she could not otherwise achieve.

Moreover, spontaneous play involves the whole body, rather than prescribing narrow patterns of movement or behavior. And this

kind of "complete" play lets a child respond to his body directly, an experience that is related to his animal nature and to his sexuality in very simple terms. Such bodily awareness can enhance a child's self-image and hence his relationship to the world around him. It's one of the few chances he gets to relate to his body, since society tends to ignore or play down this aspect of development in children.

Another important aspect of children's physical development is muscle programming, which is a function of the cerebellum of the brain. Certain basic bodily skills, such as crawling, standing erect, and walking, are the result of a child's learning to use a group of muscles for a particular function and practicing that skill until it becomes habitual. A child trying to master the use of a spoon offers a good example of muscle programming; at first he can't find his mouth and leaves bits of food on his chin or nose or clothing. But with practice he finds his mouth, gains control of the spoon, and even can focus his attention on something else while eating.

Much of muscle programming seems to come instinctively, as children's urge to crawl and later to stand suggests. One instinctive activity that requires this process of habituation is a skill called brachiation, or swinging by the arms. This is a complex skill involving momentum, rhythm, and hand-eye coordination, which children rarely attempt before age five. When a child first tries this movement, her wrists and hands bear most of her body's weight, and she moves stiffly, as if stepping, from one rung of a horizontal ladder

to the next. As she becomes accustomed to this action, her movements become more fluid and her total musculature becomes involved in the exercise. Brachiation is a trademark of many primates, and this tendency to get up in the air and swing from arm to arm is one legitimate way that kids are like monkeys.

A good playground can facilitate both simple and more sophisticated muscle programming through diversity of structures. Besides including such standard features as horizontal ladders for brachiation and ramps for eye-foot coordination, the play space can

have a "soft" environment, such as a cargo net or knotted-rope structure. The soft environment automatically adds to children's experience of movement and muscle programming because they constantly have to adjust to its changing surface and to the actions of others in the same space.

The variety of objects and surfaces in a playground also can duplicate experiences that children would ordinarily get only in a more remote natural setting. Rock climbing, for instance, requires stretching, friction, and wedging movements that help a child (or an adult) to achieve a full, vigorous physical status. Through careful planning, a community group can create a play environment that incorporates these and other experiences from nature. Still another benefit of providing for diverse experiences is that kids are thereby exposed to irregular shapes, surfaces, and materials in their everyday surroundings. Such variety certainly surpasses mere repetition of common objects, and it can literally improve the way children see the world.

LEARNING It's probably fair to say that children are learning whenever they play, though there may be as many definitions of learning as there are observers of children. But two aspects of play that unquestionably involve learning are the self-knowledge children gain from these experiences and the relationship of play to formal education.

Children use play to explore themselves and their surroundings in several ways. For one thing, they test their physical skills by playing, which develops self-confidence and teaches them to trust their judgment. For another, while playing they keep practicing something they have previously failed at until that new skill or movement is mastered.

Similarly, children participating in group play might invent or acquire whole patterns of behavior, or they may imitate adults' actions and situations. Often they are trying out new ways of relating to the world, such as being kids on a platform one minute and explorers poling down a wild river the next. Just as they need to take physical risks to grow, kids seem intuitively to know the value and the pleasure of using their imaginations.

Visual Perception

Perception is an area of psychology that has much to say about the importance of early childhood experiences. Many varied studies in this field suggest that full development of perceptual ability is dependent on environmental stimuli.

In a study that clearly demonstrates the relationship between visual perception and environmental diversity, the visual acuity of two groups of Canadian citizens was measured by scientists at Queens University in Kingston, Ontario (*Science*, November 16, 1973, pp. 729–731). One group consisted of Euro-Canadians, who lived in urban settings dominated by the straight lines and boxlike architecture of most cities. The other group was composed of Cree Indians from eastern Canada, whose environment included a variety of shapes and contours. Upon examination for visual acuity, the city-bred persons living in a "carpentered" environment showed the typical affinity for vertical and horizontal lines, as compared with oblique orientations. The Cree Indians, however, showed no special affinity for the straight vertical and horizontal lines; rather, their visual acuity was consistently good for all types of contours. This study suggests that the visual variety in environments, particularly at very young ages, permanently affects people's perceptual abilities or limitations.

Sometimes, too, children will alter their awareness, by holding their breath until they're faint, or by hanging upside down for a new look at something familiar. Such imaginary and real changes in perspective contribute to the learning process for children.

ORAL TRADITION

Written history covers only a small portion of the time that human beings have existed. And while ethologists have pointed out the importance of evolution to behavior in animals, humans have the added capacity to evolve through traditions, which are not in their genetic code, but in their culture. The means by which cultures have been preserved and developed over the long period of human existence has been through storytelling, the oral tradition.

In fact, it may be that one of our most precious skills is the capacity to tell and remember verbatim culturally relevant stories. This is the way cultures are evolved and are modified, and the process of cultural evolution through the oral tradition continues today, though it is being supplanted by mass communication as the main vehicle for cultural continuity.

Every culture has characteristic stories. Among the most interesting are those of the mystical tradition of the Middle East, the Sufi stories. Idries Shah has published a contemporary collection of the Sufi stories, which embody the wisdom and cultural heritage of Islam. These tales are especially relevant to children's development because of their humor and the general sense of playfulness about them.

Kids' impulses to investigate their environment is another facet of growth. When a child goes home from school or walks on a beach, she's all over the place, touching things, smelling, poking with her foot or a stick. This is part of a child's natural interest in what's around her, and it's the sign of a functioning, lively intelligence. Likewise, if a day-to-day setting such as the schoolyard or classroom offers a variety of experiences, the children will have lots of choices to make and their relationship to that space will remain vital.

Play can also be part of education in the traditional sense. For example, one kind of trading card that's currently popular with elementary school kids makes a joke out of some brand-name product. The name and appearance of the product are close to the real thing, but its purpose is changed to make it funny, such as disposable diapers that keep the baby wet instead of dry or a soap that dissolves things instead of cleaning them. This type of play on words is fun for kids, and at the same time teaches them word recognition and encourages their mental agility.

I don't think that kids' education stops at the classroom door. I think they learn a lot out on the playground. A lot of social learning goes on there, and it leads to an understanding of who you are and how you fit into the scene in the school. I think an educational system is a support environment, where you're trying to minimize the risk of failure, whether that failure is falling out of a jungle gym onto the asphalt or falling out of the "A" reading group into the remedial one. You want to make a support system such that if a kid fails, it's not going to ruin him.

Cognitive Growth

The theories of Jean Piaget provide a strong argument for children's having a varied and challenging environment for play. Piaget has determined that a child's cognitive growth is directly related to her ability to do things—that the child not only learns from experience, but that she must have experience in order to learn. Piaget also notes that there is a regular progression in the development of a child's conceptual capacities.

The stages of conceptual growth appear to be interdependent and to have general age equivalents in most children. Although it has not been fully established as yet, it is likely that these stages are the same for all children, but the age at which they occur may vary widely in children with neurological or other disorders.

There is an interesting relationship between the ideas of Piaget and those of Maria Montessori in that she also saw stages of development and direct experience as fundamental to cognitive growth in children. Her writings offer practical suggestions for learning situations based on these ideas. For example, she suggests giving children letters made out of sandpaper when they are first learning the alphabet, thus making the learning experience both a visual and a tactile one.

As for the role of play or the playground in the functioning of a school, it can be an integral part of children's growth and education. In addition to whatever specific knowledge a school offers children, it should ideally be a support system for them, an environment that helps each child develop and maintain his own unique self-concept. A good playground can provide an example for such a supportive environment or bolster an already existing one.

Such a support system also can help the school perform its generally accepted function of trying to create citizens who will fit into modern society. In terms of mere survival, the skills a child learns outside the classroom may be as important as the specific knowledge that is presented in the curriculum. A young person who is not particularly interested in school may retain little of the information offered to him, but he can still do many jobs well and survive quite adequately in spite of poor reading or math skills. If, on the other hand, a child has difficulty getting along with people, it will probably be a greater handicap to him than an inability to read well or to remember the multiplication tables.

While the quality and effectiveness of education vary among communities, one constant is the predominance of "book learning" in all kinds of schools. Recent studies of brain physiology, however, reveal that the two halves of the cerebral cortex have separate and distinct learning functions; the left cortex is involved with abstract-symbolic information, rather like a computer, and the right cortex takes a holis-

NONVERBAL COMMUNICATION

Learning how to behave is another important element in a child's development. Society deals harshly with people whose behavior is "different," usually by ostracizing them. For example, a slight aberration may be punished by exclusion from social activities, while a greater deviation from "normal" may result in banishment to an institution such as a mental hospital or prison.

Sociologist Erving Goffman has concentrated his studies on types of behavior as a form of communication. Goffman is particularly interested in people's social interaction, which he examines in detail in *The Presentation of Self in Everyday Life.*

Goffman points out that the unspoken attitude with which a person relates to others predisposes the response he will get. If that person tells a transparent lie in a conversation, the people with whom he is talking have to decide to let it pass or to call him on it. On the one hand, they will be uncomfortable if they continue the fabrication, and on the other hand, they may be unwilling to interrupt the superficial flow of social interaction with a confrontation. These kinds of social learning experience, and the feedback from them, are essential for children, and the play environment can provide a congenial setting for them.

tic approach, having to do with such things as imaginative thinking and musical ability.

Unfortunately, kids get great doses of the computerlike left cortical thinking and very little of the overview type of right cortical stimulation. After ten or fifteen years of using this information-processing system to the neglect of the holistic approach, a person's learning abilities could get a bit lopsided. One way to correct this imbalance in learning is to provide ample sources of stimulation for children's more imaginative side. The playground itself is an outlet for right cortical function because play, as an innate form of learning, tends to involve the whole person.

Bringing the playground into the school's curriculum also fosters a balanced form of learning. The children's education can be made more practical and at the same time more universal by creation of an outdoor classroom. One lesson, for example, could involve research into various games and athletic events, measuring distances for them on the playground, converting those figures into different systems of measurement (such as feet into meters), painting lines or otherwise marking sites for these activities, and then learning to play them.

The curriculum uses for this outdoor space are almost endless. A cargo net can become the home of reading sessions for a small group, all sorts of nature studies can be planned around the plants and animals to be found in the space, and a class could even do justice to Shakespeare, using the play structure as a stage. Other school projects could add to the play environment as well. A class might make batik banners for the play struc-

28

Brain Physiology

There are two important scientific frontiers in this modern era—the macrocosmic world of outer space and the microcosmic world of the human brain, or inner space. In the current research on physiology of the brain, scientists are verging on comprehension of how thought occurs, tracing it from sensation through interiorization and synthesis to action at the biochemical level.

What this means is that we are going to be uncovering information that will revolutionize society and thus education. Consequently, anyone who is interested in education should stay abreast of these sophisticated developments in brain physiology, for in the absence of concerned, informed opinion from educators, medical specialists may be put in the position of deciding how these developments will be applied to society. The lessons of the technological explosion and its attendant problems should show the necessity of maintaining control over the use of scientific advances.

ture, or a community's history might be depicted on one wall of the school building.

The playground also can serve as a source of information for teachers. If a teacher observes that a child who has a reading problem in class also has difficulty catching a ball on the playground, a physical deficiency that affects both coordination and reading may be uncovered. Similarly, a teacher may encounter a child who for some reason can't or won't play. In these situations, school staff members can use the playground as a diagnostic tool, and their observations may help define and then solve the learning or behavior problems of some children.

Building Play into the Environment

Play is intimately related to its environment. The atmosphere of a playground affects the way children interact and influences their feelings about themselves. The quality of the environment, too, can stimulate and enrich play experiences for kids. One way to stimulate play is by encouraging childlike behavior, such as crawling. A person of any age can be readily taken back to the experience of learning to walk simply by standing on a platform that is suspended on chains. That person will feel the same frustrating sense of imbalance and lack of control over his body as a child does when trying to stand and walk. Such experiences are both healthful and playful for children, and they also can serve as a kind of social equalizer.

LEARNING DISORDERS

Currently only persons with sophisticated training can diagnose cognitive aberrations from physical performance. It will not be long, though, before these insights will be put into a form that teachers and parents could use to detect learning disorders. The closest approach to such a refined form is offered by A. Jean Ayres in *Sensory Integration and Learning Disorders*. Her work is unique and important in that it bridges the significant gap between brain physiology and physical therapy.

A common approach to overcoming learning disorders in children has been to provide a setting that is rich in stimuli, on the assumption that something is lacking in the average environment. Recent research, however, suggests that structuring stimulation may be the way to get past a stumbling block in the child's capacity to learn. The development of alternative pathways to "normal" learning behavior, such as limiting the stimuli in an environment, is an area of much current research.

An important objective in creating a community-built playground is to give kids a sense of place. Their participation in the planning and building process helps a lot, and ideally they should also be able to change or augment the playground according to their vision. Another way of creating a sense of place in an environment for children is to scale the structures to their size. Any adult who has visited a kindergarten room full of tiny furniture, for example, knows how strange it feels to be grossly out of proportion to the surroundings; since kids are the ones who are subjected to this mismatched scale most of the time, the playground can be one place that is theirs in size as well as in name.

The sense of place likewise affects the way people relate to each other. When someone is hiking in the mountains and meets another person, there's a sort of automatic kinship between them, and friendly greetings and conversation come easily. Contrarily, if those same two people were sitting in a noisy bus station, waiting for an already late ride home from work, chances are they wouldn't feel friendly toward anyone. The trick, of course, is to make a playground seem more like the mountains than the bus station, and it's mostly a matter of attitude.

That sort of bus station attitude is still

evident in many play environments, but there are some concrete ways to change it. Usually the first playground where kids play with each other very much is in a nursery school, and quite often the principal activity is riding tricycles. If there is little else to do in that play space, the trikes become objects of competition and controversy among children, and the teacher ends up acting like a policeman. But as soon as other activities are added to the playground, such as a sandbox, a climbing structure, or a slide, the pressure is off the tricycles. Now the kids have several activities to choose among, and they are much less likely to fight over what previously had been their only source of fun, the trikes. This depressurization of the environment also relieves the teacher of the burden of policing the play space, thereby making his role there potentially more fun too.

With careful planning, a community group can create an environment that accommodates the many characteristics of play and yet fits into its space and budget. The following guidelines well help such groups increase the play potential and versatility of these community-built playgrounds.

MAXIMIZING ALTERNATIVES One way for the community to make the most efficient use of space and materials is to design a structure that offers maximum alternatives for play. Components of the play structure can be built so that kids have several choices of activity on them, such as a four-foot-wide horizontal ladder, which lets several kids go across at the same time, passing each other, with some walking on top and

some doing the traditional hand-over-hand movement. Each platform should have three exits, preferably all different, and when a child gets to the top of a structure, his choices could include a fire pole, bridge, cargo net or rope environment, chain climber, or tunnel. This kind of designing for choice suits the voluntary nature of play and also discourages such no-exit competitions as "king of the mountain," since there are always three ways for a kid to get out of a tight spot.

DOING MORE WITH LESS Similarly, the play potential of a structure is enhanced by elements that do two things at once. Platforms, for example, can be arranged in a spiral fashion so that the highest platform is directly above the lowest, saving both space and material (since one post will support a corner of four platforms in this type of design). A structural feature can also provide for a special activity. Diagonal crosspieces, called "flagging," are necessary for rigidity in some structures, but they also create a private, shaded area for the children. A play component, too, can serve two purposes, such as a slide that shelters a sand-play area. And finally, the natural features of a site can be utilized in the playground and sometimes even can form the basis for a structure, as a huge eucalyptus tree does in one neighborhood park in California.

INTEGRATING EQUIPMENT The way in which components are arranged in a play environment significantly affects the amount of enjoyment kids get there. Too often a playground will consist of isolated

DESIGN

Such concepts as doing more with less and maximizing alternatives are characteristics of good design, but how does a designer arrive at these ideas? A designer is really not so much an inventor as a discoverer. Everything that exists in life has an inherent structure; the designer discovers such structures and uses these insights to solve problems.

The quintessential designer is R. Buckminster Fuller, who might be described as a futurist and a supreme generalist. Like all designers, Fuller is always expanding his view of the world, looking for the broadest possible perspective. Fuller is especially important to contemporary society because he has brought the excitement of discovery to so many young people. The geodesic dome, Fuller's best-known design, has become a symbol for the modern era. Utilizing the basic strength of triangulation, it employs a minimal amount of material to create huge structures —something that could not be done with traditional design systems.

activities like swings, slides, and a merry-go-round, all separated by big empty spaces. This kind of arrangement keeps kids alone and apart, rather than facilitating games that involve the whole playground. If the pieces of equipment are tied together, however, children will invent games and situations around them. No longer are the activities isolated: platforms become stations, while tunnels, ladders, and bridges carry kids from one place to another. Integration of activities on a playground also allows a group to utilize whatever equipment it might already have; one parent group at a nursery school carried a two-thousand-pound concrete climber across the playground so that it could be tied into the wooden structure the parents were building.

VARIETY Kids respond to variety in a play environment. This can mean a diversity of textures, shapes, and materials, as well as activities. Surfaces can be smooth and warm, such as wood, or rough and cold, such as concrete. Shapes can be nonarchitectural, that is, not the traditional straight lines and square corners; some types of wooden structures even have graceful hyperbolic curves as a design element. Soft environments can add three-dimensional variety to a playground, such as a cargo net with a rope spiderweb above it. These soft areas give kids new physical experiences, especially when someone else moves unexpectedly, and they are uniquely comfortable places to be.

SELF-LIMITING STRUCTURES
Another approach to planning a playground

for children of different ages is to build self-limiting structures. A grouping of elements of the same form but of various sizes accomplishes this goal, since the different sizes complement children's natural tendency to find their own physical limits. This gradation of skills can also be arranged in a large structure by having small-scale activities at one end or side and more difficult, larger elements at the other. One important consideration in this type of arrangement, though, is providing adequate ways for smaller kids to get off the structure before they go beyond their own limits.

The natural spaces we have should be preserved. And they can only be preserved if we kind of depressurize the space and get the kids enough to do so that they lay off the living things. You can't get a natural stream and bushes and an ecology area going until you give them some kind of active-play center and someplace where they can have some privacy, or they'll be trying to get privacy in the bushes that you're trying to protect.

PROTECTING NATURAL AREAS

Since they usually must support hundreds of children, playgrounds take quite a beating. But if there is sufficient equipment to keep the kids occupied, the trees, plants, and even grass in the same area have a chance to survive. Where even the play equipment will take a beating from constant, heavy use, natural experiences might be duplicated in extremely strong forms, such as a welded "tree" made from auto exhaust pipes. This apparatus offers the same climbing challenges as a tree but in a lateral direction, so a kid moves fifteen feet sideways instead of straight up.

Once an environment has been depressurized by an active-play center, a group can create a nature area that has more chance to flourish. Besides, the provision of energy-absorbing active-play areas to allow for coexistence of natural things can be a good approach to giving children some practical environmental awareness. And, at least indirectly, the creation of compatible play structures and natural areas may help to preserve the wilderness that remains on our continent. If these small parks can relieve some of the urban pressures, perhaps people will feel less compelled to get away to the ever-shrinking woods.

2 Can We Do It?

It's my contention that playgrounds can only be built by community people. Creating an environment that stimulates play and supports kids' good feelings about themselves is so complex that the only way we can really handle it is intuitively. When we take our native intelligence and our feelings about ourselves and our kids and put them together intuitively, we make an expression that is both a conscious and unconscious act which reflects who we think we are, where we want to go, what our dreams are. You're not going to get that with a set of plans, a hard-hat crew, and a jackhammer; it just doesn't happen that way. We're back to "the medium is the message," the basic idea that what you do is what you've got. And if there's an alternative to the juggernaut of concrete, it's not going to be more bulldozers—it's going to be people.

The Usual Standards Don't Apply

Perhaps because play is strictly voluntary, it can't be treated like a commodity, nor its environment sold to the lowest bidder. There is no professional solution for play, no team of experts who can construct a playground

that has the personal, caring qualities of a community's collective efforts.

An environment derives its essence from the way it is fashioned and the way it is used, and, for a playground at least, some of the usual standards don't apply. Take money, for instance. A contractor couldn't build for $10,000 what a group of parents and kids can do for half that. And although a contractor would be efficient and his execution of the plans might be perfect, efficiency and perfection are not so important here. Indeed, it's the nicks and scratches, the awkwardness that comes from learning while doing, that gives a community-built playground its identity and charm.

Similarly, a community group has different criteria for designing a playground than most professional designers or builders are accustomed to using. The parents at a school with little or no money for a playground have to find ways to use the leftovers, such as old tires, peeler cores (the remnants of making plywood), cable spools, or trees that were cut

down to make room for a highway. If the design is based on whatever materials the group has hustled, it's not likely to be the type of job a contractor is used to handling. Or a particularly adventuresome community may just assemble all the materials its members can find, then start to build without any formal plans. What they'll probably get will be a structure that resembles nothing else in the world, plus a lot of practical experience at solving problems on the spot and a very special set of feelings about their space.

This is not to say that professionals such as contractors cannot build playgrounds, but rather to emphasize that anybody can do it. There are hundreds of community-built playgrounds to support that assertion, built by people at all levels of society, in all kinds of places. Jay Beckwith's clients, for instance, have included nursery schools, public and private elementary schools, parks and recreation departments of cities and towns, and special centers, including a state hospital for retarded persons and a school for deaf children. Although his business is centered in

San Francisco, Beckwith regularly travels the seven counties of the Bay Area and has worked with groups as far away as San Diego and Los Angeles.

Practical Considerations

Once a community group has decided to go ahead with the playground, it is often eager to start building the next day or weekend. But a project of this size requires a good deal of preparation, and sometimes more negotiation than anyone imagined. Of course the members will need this interim for planning, scrounging materials, and so forth, and it's also an appropriate time for them to review their goals for the community and the children.

In addition to the specific information about how kids play and how to plan effectively for it, Beckwith has several general reminders for the groups with whom he works. First, this project is for the children, and they should be involved in it from the beginning. Also, the community members should always think beyond the immediate task. This project is not just planning and building a structure; it's establishing a process of change. They should think of their play environment as perpetually unfinished, and since they'll have mastered the skills by building one structure, they will be able to keep the process going on their own. And finally, this process of playground creation is a way of changing attitudes, about play, about what a school should be, about people taking control over their environment.

Making changes in the common spaces of a community is by nature a political activity, and to make a political change you have to have money or people, or both. So if the community wants to express a change in a space, they need to have lots of people involved in the most realistic fashion possible, which in this case is working on the site, preparing to exercise their control over it. One person out there working, talking to his neighbors and visible to everybody, is worth ten people who send checks. And to a politician, fifty people who are deeply involved in such an effort translate into a thousand votes, because of their impact on the whole community.

SITE Sometimes getting the space for a playground is the biggest hurdle in the project. If community members seek to use a part of their common space, such as a public

park or school, they will find that some existing government machinery nominally has authority over it. Quite often, these lines of authority aren't clear, and individuals in the system may be reluctant to make any firm commitment to the community group. But people who think they ought to have some right of approval over the project will practically come out of the woodwork.

Of course the particular problems of a group's working its way successfully through

the government machinery will differ in each community, but the experience of people who've already built playgrounds can offer some useful examples. First, a community group probably will have to make its case at every point in the line of authority, and it's important to hold out consistently for the community's right to decide how this space should be used. The people should determine the aesthetics of their common spaces, since they must live with these environments, and they should likewise have a role in determining the function of and access to such areas. The actual owners of a space, however, are liable if injuries or damage occurs there. Consequently, the group must convince the government or other owner that the environment created by the community will be a safe and beneficial one.

Numbers help, and for creation of playgrounds, kids help a lot. They can talk up the project to their parents, give presentations at meetings of local organizations, and maybe set up an information booth at the public library. And if lots of children and parents appear at meetings of the government body that must approve the project, it will clearly demonstrate the community's support for the playground. Another strong point is that this project, after all, is for the children, and at the most basic level, who can object to a place for kids to play?

Once a group has gotten jurisdiction over a specific place, and that may not always be a struggle, the site must be made ready for a playground. Whatever the final plans for the environment, the area for an active-play center must be relatively flat, with adequate

drainage. If the space is covered with asphalt, it can be broken up and removed, or a structure and soft ground cover can rest on top of it.

Even fairly simple site preparation can be expensive, and it will eat up an inordinate amount of a group's budget if it has to pay for this work. The fact that the people are doing this on their own, however, provides good leverage for getting the local parks or public works department to do this preparation. Or the group might solicit help from a local builder or from military reserve groups or the National Guard, since many of these groups have the heavy equipment that is usually needed for this job.

MONEY   Much of the fun and sense of accomplishment in a community's building a playground comes from doing it on a shoestring. Frugality may get the builders plenty of mileage for future projects as well, since most government officials will not just be impressed that the group built this environment for, say, $1,500—they'll be astounded.

Like getting access to a site, finding money for the playground takes persistence and imagination, but it can certainly be done. This kind of fund raising benefits from the clear image that the group can present simply by saying, "We're building our own playground and we need some help." Among the sources that community groups have tapped are federal, state, and local funds, as well as private donations from foundations or individuals. One group of parents at an especially poor co-op nursery school got a promise of government funds if it could come up with a matching amount. The parents had very little cash, but they figured the value of their donated labor at $2.50 per hour and used that "sum" to satisfy the matching requirement.

In San Francisco a group of public elementary schools made a joint proposal and got federal revenue-sharing funds for seventeen schoolyard improvement projects. After five of these projects were completed and most others were under way, a city government committee decided to reevaluate its allocation of revenue-sharing money, thus putting the schoolyard funds in jeopardy. When the government committee met to decide which funds to cut off, however, the meeting room was filled with parents and children, who had brought models, drawings, and blueprints of their schools' projects. The committee heard the group's presentation, voted to continue giving funds to the school group, and even promised to eliminate some of the paperwork involved in keeping the projects going.

Other groups have raised money in the community through traditional methods, such as bake sales and athletic events. At some elementary schools the kids have voted their funds for the playground, a tactic that has usually shamed their elders into contributing too. One group that didn't have a

built-in community, such as a school or neighborhood, raised money for a playground at the San Francisco County jail by exhibiting a model of the playground and seeking donations. Again, kid power is quite useful for raising funds; there's something irresistible about an eight-year-old showing her drawing and explaining what her playground will be like.

Although there are many variables, such as availability and prices of lumber in different areas, some general estimates can be made for the cost of a playground (not including site preparation or fencing). For big elementary schools, a good yardstick is $1,000 per hundred children, and if we assume that the playground is good for ten years (which is a conservative estimate), that's a dollar per kid per year. A school with only 100 kids, however, probably will need at least $1,500 to $2,000 to build a good environment. Similarly, a nursery school may have 50 children, but a complete playground for the school could cost $2,000. These estimates are based on the average costs of playgrounds built by community groups working with Jay Beckwith, but other playgrounds he has helped create have cost as little as $300 and as much as $10,000.

Another way to plan for a playground is to decide what portion of the budget will be used for its various elements. Beckwith advises his clients that they will use about 30 per cent of their budget for his services, which include giving several workshops for adults and children, helping them to put their ideas into design form, preparing drawings, blueprints, or a model (and sometimes all three), and providing all the tools and direction they'll need on workdays. The advantage of hiring a consultant for the project, Beckwith points out, is that the group gets an experienced person who can make decisions and who will be responsible for keeping the project going at a good pace and seeing that it gets finished, something that an unpaid coordinator may not have the time or influence to accomplish. Ground cover can absorb another 25 per cent of the budget, with the other 45 per cent going for lumber, hardware, and equipment. Another consideration is commercial equipment, which often can be built into the structure and may save in time what it costs in dollars.

MATERIALS Putting together the makings of a playground can be an exercise in discovering community resources. Since most groups have small budgets and big intentions, whatever breaks they can get in gathering materials will help. One approach to saving money on materials that must be bought is to order them through someone who gets a discount, such as a nonprofit organization or the school district. The group might also be able to talk local merchants into donating supplies or selling them at wholesale prices. A contractor who has projects in the neighborhood might be willing to donate or order supplies at a discount, a mother in one community group observed, just to keep the kids off his building site and equipment.

Scrounging materials can likewise be developed into an art, and a playground has great potential for use of leftovers and castoffs. Some likely sources of interesting and inexpensive materials are government surplus and salvage stores, scrap-metal dealers, state and federal surplus outlets (which often have catalogs), and utility companies. Items that are often available for free include trees (in various forms) from park or highway departments or builders who are clearing sites; tires of all sizes from tire dealers (possibly old inner tubes too); telephone poles or the short end pieces from them from the power and phone companies; and possibly railroad ties from railroad yards. Peeler cores, which are eight-foot-long round logs left from plywood production, may be available at lumber mills; they can be cheaper than most other lumber. Cable spools are another popular item, but recently

one utility company refused to give its extra ones to a community group for a playground because the spools are no longer made of top-quality wood, and the company didn't want to jeopardize the kids or its own reputation.

PLANNING   In a sense, everything to do with a playground is part of the planning, but there are some definite guidelines that can help a community group generate the most appropriate design for its needs. First, a group should have some knowledge of the alternatives to the traditional type of playground. If there are other community-built structures in the vicinity, visits to them (with the kids, naturally) will be very useful. The group might also consult library resources or university architecture or planning departments for ideas and possibly for a consultant who specializes in play environments.

Based on its research into the types of structures it might build, a group may wish to decide on one type of design, A-frame, for example, and gear its fund-raising and material-gathering efforts to that plan. It's more likely, though, that the members will reserve decision on the specific design until they've gathered more information. In this case an important factor in their planning will be the types of materials that are available in their area and within reach of their budget.

Whether or not a group has chosen a type of design, it will need certain information to determine the exact size of the structure and the kinds of activities to be provided in the space. The children, parents, and staff (if it's a school) should be canvassed regarding the types of equipment they want for the playground. This preliminary information also should include a map of the playground site, showing the dimensions of the space and all topographical features, such as trees, uneven ground, and so forth. Patterns of traffic through the space also must be noted, with an indication of whether or not the flow of movement might be rerouted if necessary.

Such observation of the playground site

can also uncover other potential problems. At one school, for instance, the traffic pattern included a garbage truck, which drove across the playground once a day to pick up garbage from the cafeteria. Although the truck came at a time when kids weren't using the playground, its daily presence precluded construction of any large structure. Of course the parents and teachers at the school were not about to let their playground be spoiled by a garbage truck, so they found a way to send it around another side of the building.

Although design types and equipment are discussed in detail in Chapters 4 and 5, some general considerations may be helpful here. The ideal situation, of course, would be for a group to provide everything possible in the play environment: an active-play structure, landscaping, a nature area, an outdoor classroom. And a group should try to plan for such a comprehensive environment, even though it will have to be built in stages. Assuming that time and money limit what can be done on the site, the most important thing to provide for the kids is an active-play center. With careful planning, this structure can accommodate the three major types of play, that is, active, climbing, and quiet play (for details, see Chapter 5). If there is not an outlet for active play, which includes such things as swings, slides, and ball games, the children will seek other, less beneficial ways to expend their energy. Imagine what would happen, for example, if a single tree were put in the middle of an empty schoolyard.

The age and size of children who will use the playground also must be taken into account. Besides the obvious correlation be-

tween their size and the scale of the play structure, children of different ages have varying needs and preferences for play activities (see chart, p. 125). Certain safety features should be built in for very young children. For example, a child of two or three doesn't yet have the cognitive ability to know that a swing that goes up and out of his field of vision is going to come back down. So this child might wander into the path of such a swing and get clobbered. To avoid this danger, swings can be designed to move in a relatively small radius so that they will stay within a young child's visual range.

When Beckwith meets with a group to begin formulating specific plans for the playground, he suggests several rules of procedure that will help people get ideas across without confusion or bad feelings. First, when commenting on an idea, a person should say two things he likes about it before criticizing it. To make his ideas more easily understood by the group, a person should try to draw a picture of what he means. (It's amazing how involved everybody gets in this.) And everyone should keep in mind that he can only solve a problem after he has all the facts.

Another important consideration is that something can almost always be changed. People may feel left out of the process if they don't have a chance to make some small change or addition to the plan. This is especially true for the dissenters, the people who don't like what other members of the group have proposed or who perhaps don't even want to see a playground built. If these persons are urged to give their suggestions or to explain their objections, the whole group may arrive at a better solution to its problems than if the unhappy few are ignored.

A group may also have a member or friend who is an architect or designer by profession and who is interested in helping plan the playground. Such informed assistance is useful, to be sure, but the group must be very careful not to let one person's aesthetics or preferences dominate its thinking. If the design turns out to be that designer's statement rather than a collective expression, the playground probably will not reflect the community's spirit.

After the group has compiled everyone's

suggestions and assessed the needs to be met by this new environment, the actual designing usually comes easily. One way to move from a list of ideas to a final design is to start putting the information on a map of the space. With a bit of experimenting, such as moving a swing from one corner to another, shifting the structure's position to provide better shelter from the wind, or combining two activities to make room for both, the playground begins to take shape on the map and in people's minds.

From here a group can take either a casual or a more formal approach to the construction of the playground. If the members want to allow for a great deal of spontaneity in the building, they can make general layouts of the structure and components to determine what materials to order, but leave the door open for changes. Other groups may prefer more precise plans and so could have blueprints drawn (although it takes some skill to interpret them on site) or make a scale model. In fact, such detailed representations are often required by authorities who must approve the structure, such as school administrators or park officials.

Making a model can be good practice for construction, and it can also solve design problems that couldn't be visualized in drawings. One of Beckwith's early play structures is a series of truncated tetrahedrons made of railroad ties and plywood end pieces. Only one of these units is equilateral; the sides of the others had to be cut at precise angles determined by the length of each piece. After working with two mathematicians and failing to find a formula

for these complex angles, Jay was finally able to determine the angle at which to cut each member of the units by experimenting with scale models of the figures.

BUILDING   Putting the playground together is what makes all the hours of meetings and phone calls pay off, and it's an opportunity for everyone in the community to participate. The kids will be there, of course, and there are plenty of jobs they can do. And playground building surely squelches the myth that women can't do much with tools, since Beckwith estimates that 80 per cent of his work crews have been women. There are usually some men who have experience in construction as well; they should be utilized to teach their skills to the rest of the group.

Workdays are generally on weekends, since those are the only days most parents and school staff members can participate. An adequate work force is ten adults and ten kids, although most work sessions will have many more people, and if necessary, five adults could comprise a minimum crew. If there are fewer than five people, however, the initial framing will be impossible to do safely, since the materials are generally too heavy and bulky to handle.

Workdays are most efficient when there has been sufficient preparation and a good routine has been established on site. The coordination required before a workday includes getting materials to the site, which means some decisions must be made about what to build on which days. This doesn't necessarily limit spontaneity while building,

but it insures that lumber will be delivered before ground cover, for example. But even the best planning can go awry. One group of parents at a nursery school arranged to have the sand they needed for ground cover delivered on a weekday so that they wouldn't have to waste work time waiting for it to arrive. The school was located in a small park between two streets, and the truck carrying the sand came in on the street next to the school building instead of the one next to the playground. The driver went past the school to where its two bordering streets intersected and tried to turn around there, but he must have pushed the wrong button because he dumped his twelve-ton load of sand in the middle of the intersection. A teacher quickly phoned the man who was in charge of the parents' committee, but he couldn't do much about twelve tons of sand in the street, so he called the city parks department, who called public works, who sent out a tractor with a scoop to clean up the mess.

Preparations for a workday also include arranging to have plenty of tools, a good selection of hardware, and electrical outlets and extension cords for the work crew, which may necessitate renting some of the bigger power tools that members of the group don't own. People should be told to bring gloves and a hammer, measuring tape, and whatever other tools they have. The crew members will also need to bring lunches with them, or the group might arrange for a community organization or local restaurant to bring food and beverages for the midday break.

The workday routine that Beckwith has found most efficient begins with an instruc-

tion session in tool use and safety. Since there probably will be new people or new skills at each phase of construction, this session should be scheduled for every workday. Another thing to be done before the day's building is checking the plans to determine what to do first, or making plans if none were prepared in advance. This on-the-spot design can be very rewarding, if a bit scary at first, and Beckwith even claims to have let the model of a playground fall off his truck on the way to the site just to give people an opportunity for such spontaneous problem solving. When the parts to be built are decided upon, a list of jobs can be posted and the crew can begin work. If there are lots of children around and few jobs for them, they might be given their own on-the-spot problem to solve, such as digging a hole and filling it in again. (They hit water this way on one playground.)

Lunch is an important part of the day because it gives everybody a chance to see what has been accomplished as a group. While people are comparing notes (and probably blisters) and renewing their energy, they can also map out the afternoon's work, perhaps changing their original plans to suit an unanticipated circumstance. At the end of each workday, the group should clean up or cover any loose material, since a pile of stones, for example, might mean some broken windows before the next weekend. Tools likewise should be returned and unused supplies stored where they won't interfere with other activities.

The end of a workday sometimes has its surprises too. One crew's first project on a particular Sunday was to build a deck from

the school's double front doors to the far side of the playground. The deck was a bit too high, though, and the doors wouldn't open, so the workers removed the doors, intending to cut a little off the bottom edge of each one. But they got busy with the other tasks scheduled for the day, and nobody remembered the doors until it was dark, they all were dead tired, and the school had to be locked up for the night. Two men stayed behind and trimmed and rehung the doors by the dim light inside the building. On the next workday they made a list of the day's unfinished jobs and checked everything off well before evening.

When Beckwith works with community groups, he recommends that they have one person on site to supervise and coordinate the building, preferably someone who has construction experience and can teach tool use and safety. Although a group is not obligated to hire him or one of his assistants, Jay does

suggest that the supervisor be someone who is not a group member because it's easier on everyone if the person who hollers at them for doing something wrong is an outsider. A hard-driving foreman also can be helpful in getting the job done as quickly as possible, since the interim while the playground is under construction is especially hard on the kids. And the children shouldn't be allowed to play on the structure until it's finished, as they tend to play more frantically than usual on a new playground, and a burst of activity on an incomplete structure might result in someone's being hurt.

When somebody asks if a structure might fall down or something, I say, "Look, we're going to be doing it out there, and we're going to be sitting on the lumber, you and I, and if you don't feel it's strong enough, we can put another brace on it. It's a decision we can make moment by moment, and listen, if it'll support ten of us adults on it, jumping up and down, it'll support those kids. And we don't have to come up with a structure that's absolutely stable; it can wiggle. We're not going to plumb it, we're not going to install windows, so the standard is different. And it doesn't have to meet any kind of codes other than our own decision about strength."

Most community-built playgrounds tend to be somewhat overbuilt because the people who plan them want to be sure to create strong enough structures for several hundred kids. One source of strength is the size of lumber used; another is the basic design use of triangulation for support. Yet another design precaution is that each component has several points of support so that if one joint fails or a bolt breaks, that part just sort of sags but doesn't come crashing down.

On the playgrounds for which Beckwith has been responsible, the rate of injuries is very low. One person was cut when using a chisel, though he was not hurt seriously, and one child broke his leg when he fell through a climber made of tires. These have been the only major mishaps, although there will always be the unavoidable bumps and scrapes. Nor have there been any major structural failures. Some adjustments have been required, of course, such as resetting the eye bolts that hold up a cargo net or replacing chain that has worn thin, but the community group usually makes these minor changes without any problems. Some groups, in fact, have gone on to build additions to the playground or initiate other construction projects on their own.

The playground-building experience has given community groups the confidence and skills to take on new projects, and the workdays have also offered many people a new perspective on their neighborhood and their neighbors. There's something about getting dirty and feeling proud of it, of coming together for the good of the children, that erases the usual barriers or pretenses that

54

people may bring into a situation. When parents and kids work together on the playground, their conventional roles disappear, and it seems very much as if they're playing. That good feeling, that sense of having fun at hard work, is one of the special by-products of this process. When it happens, when work and play seem to merge, everybody feels it. Laughter and conversation compete with the din of hammers, drills, and power saws, and at the end of the day people go home smiling tired.

INVOLVING THE KIDS Besides helping on workdays, the children who will use the playground should be in on the planning from the start. They're the logical ones, for example, to suggest a place for the playground because they know the neighborhood intimately. And kids should be encouraged to give their suggestions for the design and activities for the structure, but unless they are exposed to some new ideas, the children may just say they want swings and slides. Kids can do a lot of the research

needed for planning, however, and find out what they might want in their own environment while doing so.

Particularly if the playground is for a school, a series of workshops could be set up for the children to make their participation an important ingredient in the process. They could visit other playgrounds, see slide presentations of community-built environments, and then begin working with their own ideas. Kids also can make the topographical and traffic-pattern maps of their space and give programs about the playground to the community at large. Other useful workshop sessions could be in drawing their ideas and then turning the drawings into models, which gives them practical experience in what building is like.

Being involved in the playground process often leaves a lasting impression on children, and evidence of this crops up unexpectedly. A classic example is the five-year-old girl who was in on all the planning and workdays because her mother was coordinator for the school's playground. Several weeks after the playground had been completed, the girl went to visit her grandmother, and at some point they began to talk about the Biblical story of the creation. When the grandmother had finished telling how God had created the earth and seas and plants and animals in six days, the five-year-old sat quietly for a few moments, then proclaimed, "God couldn't have made the world in six days. It takes a weekend to make a playground."

Kids' visions of what things are can be implemented; they're real. And their vision, their

kind of unique, special culture should be allowed to exist.

In some places, too, the kids can do all the planning and most of the building. At one park in a poor section of the city, the kids helped make a free-form village out of cement, plastered it, and then painted it, all without prior planning or restraint from any adults. The only problem, Beckwith recalls, was that half the time he'd have to send the kids home to change clothes because they'd come all dressed up.

In certain ways, children have no respect; they'll very carefully make a design of mosaics in the plaster covering of a cement structure and then paint a face right on top of the mosaics, something an adult would never do. But the kids do take care of what is theirs. As one high school student at a community meeting put it: "It seems like with most of these parks they spend more money fixing them up than building them, 'cause when kids don't help make it they don't care what happens to it."

INCLUDING THE COMMUNITY

Most groups who are planning to build their own playgrounds want people to know about them so that everyone who's interested has a chance to participate. And once people have been involved in such a project, they're eager to help others get started. Being able to share this experience is one good reason for group members to document their entire project. They will then be able to make presentations to other groups who want to create play environments. Several groups might also pool their information and create a resource center for playgrounds, as a San Francisco group has done.

The residents of the San Francisco area also had an unusually good opportunity to participate in the community-built-playground process during a six-week exhibit at the M. H. de Young Memorial Museum in the city. This show, which featured the work of Jay Beckwith, included daily workshops for school children and a community building project during which volunteers constructed the framework for a playground behind the museum. One room in the museum also became a "soft environment," with wooden seats hung from above on ropes and set into a cargo net, where people sat to watch a six-image slide show of the whole playground process. Anyone who stayed for five minutes went away with a sensation of what it's like to build and to play in such an environment.

In a word, the thing that happens between people when they work together, particularly when they work together to create play, is magic. It's really invisible what happens. People go away with a feeling of it. There's a sense of accomplishment, a sense of fulfillment, a sense of having done something, but if you would ask them what happened, they couldn't tell you. They would say, "Well, I learned something," or, "We built something," but they really wouldn't be able to begin to touch that thing that they're feeling.

"I feel that our city is responsive to the citizens. I've never seen anyone who came in and said, 'We'll do this; will you help us?' turned down. So it becomes a team, a community effort of the citizens, the city council, and the department staff to get this park built. I've seen more excitement on this one park than on any other area in town. This is just people in the community, pulling together for this one thing. And they had everyone from little kids up to grandparents out there working on it." (City park and recreation director)

"I had ten women bosses yesterday. I dug postholes, and one woman said, 'No, you've got to go two feet,' and one said, 'You've got to go six inches,' and another said, 'Get out of here—my nail is straight; it's not crooked.'" (Father)

"If you can't provide your children with a natural environment, like a farm or a forest, where they can do all the experimenting and everything on their own, then I think this is the next best thing to doing that. There are all kinds of ways they can use that playground. They're not just climbing; they're not just moving their front leg muscles to go up some steps to swoosh down something. They have that experience, but there's a whole lot of other things too. There are hiding places in that playground, really neat ones. The kids really take delight in that—it's a whole environment." *(Mother who was a school volunteer)*

"The feeling that you have when you wake up in the morning and you know you're going down to work is really exciting. I could parallel it to a feeling that I used to get when I was a kid on the farm, in September, when we'd pick apples. And I remember waking up as a kid and putting on heavy underwear and heavy clothes, and every time I'd put something on I'd think, 'And this is to keep me warm.' I'd pretend I was some settler coming across the Great Divide. I'd get out there and it was cold, and still almost dark, and everything was really exciting. And that's the way it was when I woke up to go building too. It was a big adventure." *(Mother of two)*

"*Most importantly, it's great for the kids. But also, it's an ideal of all the years I've been teaching, which is nine in this school. It's the first real community project where parents, students, and teachers all really could work together as a group.*" (*Teacher and father*)

"And for those of us who kept coming back every weekend, we got really efficient. Everything was always in the same place, and we got to know what tools were in what boxes, and how to use them. And learning to use those power tools—that was really a thrill for me. It's really exciting to build. Like I would be chiseling, notching to put in a side guardrail or something, and it takes forever to do that. And some guy would come along with his big muscles and say, 'Here, let me do that for you.' And I'd say, 'No, no. I'm doing this.' It was really a place for us to assert ourselves. The women in the group all felt the same way, and I think it was really a healthy experience for us. We've talked about that, having a chance to go do something different like that." (Woman who was there every workday)

"We need a washer—you know, one of those squashed things with a hole in it, like a metal donut." (Foreman to six-year-old boy)

"Something that we could make, lumpy though it may be, will be better because we made it—at least we'll think so." (Principal of city elementary school)

3 What's So Special Here?

A creative playground is only half a creative space; it's also a creative attitude. And we're changing attitudes as much as we're changing spaces. It's that willingness of a parent to stand back and let a kid hold the drill, or of an experienced builder to let someone else make a mistake, to be proud of his ability to teach instead of his ability to do. Those kinds of attitudes are the ones we develop first.

What About Vandalism?

Community-built playgrounds differ from traditional ones in a number of ways, but perhaps the most telling evidence of a playground's value to the community is its staying power. Vandalism has long been an expectation among school administrators and park officials, and their answer usually is to build fortresslike structures that defy destruction. Unfortunately, defiance is quite often the attitude these places inspire in kids, who then go to elaborate lengths to prove their superiority over concrete and steel. In other words, the playgrounds that are planned with vandalism in mind get just that.

If children are treated with trust and respect, on the other hand, they are much more likely to give back those attitudes. When

their parents and teachers consult them about what the playground should be, and then build it with them, the kids are going to treasure and protect that space. Instead of doing harm to their environment, in fact, the children will be able to add to it, perhaps by painting certain surfaces or making a knotted-rope climber.

The community-built playgrounds that Jay Beckwith has helped create have had very little vandalism. Some rope was stolen from one, and people have added spray-can art to some places. Beckwith is reluctant to call this adornment vandalism, but prefers

the term "creative self-expression," since he sees it as kids trying to make their presence felt in the environment.

The opportunity for children to make their presence felt, in fact, is the chief characteristic of adventure playgrounds, which flourish in England and Europe, but have existed only as short-term experiments in this country. Although these playgrounds have adult supervision, they are truly child-centered environments, where the kids can build their own structures, tear them down, dam up a creek or dig a pond, and even learn to fight a fire they've started.

My feeling is that when you put a kid out in an asphalt playground, that space says to the child, "We don't care about you as a person. You're going to be here for a while, and you're going to pass on, and this school is not going to change." And since that says to a child that no one cares about him, the child then feels, "Well, why should I care about myself?" And he becomes care-less.

Maintenance is another factor that weighs heavily on the bureaucratic mind and thus influences the way a playground looks and feels. And conveniently for these planners, the concrete-and-steel "solution" to vandalism also is easy to maintain; it can just be hosed down. Such places, however, are not necessarily easy on the kids. If they are trying to do damage to the playground, or even hurting themselves out there, the children are saying in kidlike ways that they're unhappy in that environment.

So it comes down to the attitudes of people who create these environments and the questions they ask when they do it. Some-

ADVENTURE PLAYGROUNDS

The rich and varied adventure playgrounds, where kids take charge of the space and the materials in it, have not as yet caught on in this country. One reason is that most public-owned areas such as schools and parks must have insurance, and insurance underwriters haven't had experience with child-controlled environments and therefore will not write policies for them, in spite of the European experience of substantially reduced accident rates in adventure playgrounds. And while American society does have an equivalent of the adventure playground in summer camp, it's unfortunate that most communities do not have the choice of creating such play environments for year-round use in the city.

One playground designer who has been working to incorporate the features of adventure playgrounds into children's environments is Robin Moore. Moore has published three booklets on his ideas and experience; all of these publications have a kidlike feeling that is reminiscent of the atmosphere of a child-centered playground. These booklets are listed in the bibliography.

where along the way the administrators and officials have gotten it backwards. This space isn't here for the convenience of custodians or as the first line of defense in a continuous battle between authorities and upstart kids. The reason for a playground is the children. If the people who share that conviction are able to take responsibility for the space, they will make an environment that responds to the real questions: what do our children need to be healthy and safe? And what do they want?

The differences in attitude between a community group and the "downtown people" often surface during the planning of a playground, and once aired, these problems are easier to overcome. In one small suburban city, for example, community members applied for part of the government's park and recreation budget to buy materials for a playground they would build themselves. They then presented their plans at a city council meeting, showing drawings of their proposed playground and explaining that they had hired Jay Beckwith to work with them as a consultant. The council was receptive to the idea, but one member just couldn't understand why the community wanted to do the work. He objected to their hiring an outside consultant, since the town had its own park planner, but the community group insisted on working with Beckwith. So the councilman stated rather sarcastically that if Beckwith was such an expert on playgrounds, why didn't the group just hire him as a contractor and let him build it? One father's response summed up the neighborhood philosophy in a sentence: "The

diminished variety and high populations, such as an urban neighborhood or a crowded public school, are indicative of communities under stress. Increasing variety in the surroundings helps to minimize the stress, though, and the playground is a place where everyone in the community can contribute to this diversity. A structure built of round logs, a tree (even though it's dead and set in cement), and the bright, unmistakably childlike paintings of butterflies and smiling faces, for instance, are an especially welcome sight to people who are otherwise surrounded by brick, cement, glass, and steel.

A group of people building a playground is a nonthreatening way of tackling the whole question of how you really do create environmental

playground might be more kidlike if Jay built it himself, but it wouldn't mean any more to us than if the downtown people built it." They got their money.

Yet another reason why play environments should be something besides asphalt and metal is that, in cities at least, there are already far too many cold, hard surfaces. What kids need is a compensatory environment, since they don't have the opportunity to live in a natural way. Environments that have

change. One of the things that the ecologists really don't understand about what they're doing is that they're going at altering the environment through specialization. And that's not the point; it's not going to make the change. What we have to do is let each person feel that he has control over the environment. So what happens when people make playgrounds is that they start looking at the classrooms and they say, "Oh, wouldn't it be nice if we had a reading loft?" Or, "Wouldn't it be nice if we got rid of these desks and let everybody sit on the floor?" Or, "Wouldn't it be nice if we opened up the doors and had a

garden outside?" And they do those things, because if they've built their own playground, they can do them.

A Legacy of Community Change

A community's building a playground can have an impact far beyond that one space. Besides meeting the immediate needs for children's play and growth, the experience has some other important results. It allows some people to learn that they can build something with their own hands, or for a person who has built before, it offers the opportunity of using and sharing her skills. And it gives people the experience, whatever their degree of sophistication, of changing a part of their environment by working together. That need, both to know that change is possible and to be able to accomplish change, is growing as the pressures of urban life grow, as governments get harder to reach and less responsive, as services diminish and options dwindle. As the community's frustration with petitioning a government increases, the impulse for action also grows, and this playground-creation process is one outlet for action, one real way of making change happen.

Once the community has begun the process of change, its pattern of action and energy spreads. Many parents will remain involved in the school, perhaps in ways related to the playground, such as planning a nature-study area, or perhaps in other ways, such as influencing curriculum or acting as tutors. Other people may use the contacts made while working on the playground to help a political candidate, for instance, or to get bicycle paths for their area.

The playground-creation process also can be mutually beneficial for neighbors and kids. One man who lived across the street from a nursery school where the parents and staff were building a playground came by on a workday and asked them if they would like an old rowboat he had behind his house. The kids immediately shouted their enthusiasm, of course, and the work crew went over and carried the somewhat battered but sound boat back to the playground, where it has passengers most of the time.

in a small elementary school, the kids not only have built their own indoor and outdoor structures, but they've also set up building codes and environmental standards for changes in their space.

In at least one instance, too, the playground has been the proverbial last straw that forced resolution of a conflict between parents and staff members at a school. The parent group at one school had been especially active in getting funds and arranging work crews for the playground's construction, and felt strongly that it would provide an important new curriculum resource for the school, in addition to enhancing the heretofore limited play environment for the children. After this large,

Kids respond to change, and they value their space. One of the ways I can tell this is I'll go back to a playground and they all recognize me. I went back to a playground I built three years ago, and the kids took me over and showed me where their painting was still on. You know, that's a remarkable thing, to leave a little bit of your identity on the space you live in. It's very unlike modern society, which tends to erase all evidence of human occupation.

The environment often continues to change in schools where the community has built the playground. Many groups have added new components to the structures, and one big elementary school recently doubled the size of its already large playground. At a child care co-op, the staff planned and built a play environment with Beckwith, then borrowed his tools a few weeks later to do extensive remodeling inside the center. And

diversified structure was completed, however, some staff members began voicing their previously unstated objections, and the playground became a source of tension between parents and staff, with the kids caught in the middle. Ultimately the situation was resolved, with a few staff members transferring to other schools, some parents working more directly with teachers and administrators, and a hard-won spirit of cooperation between the two groups.

PLAY AND CULTURE

One of the most famous theories of play is that of Johan Huizinga, whose *Homo Ludens* (Man the Player) sets forth his idea that "civilization arises and unfolds in and as play." Huizinga believed that play is not just an element in culture, but that it actually predates and is fundamental to culture. As ethologists have demonstrated since the publication of *Homo Ludens* (in 1938), animals play instinctively, and playful behavior existed long before human beings organized themselves into societies.

One of Huizinga's more startling ideas is that play forms the basis for religious experience. The theorist points out that play is often performed in seriousness and earnest and that the players are transported to another world or state of consciousness—precisely the characteristics of religious ritual. Like ritual, play also occurs in a separate and distinct place, whether that place is set off by actual or imaginary boundaries. And finally, in both play and the fundamental rites of a religion, spiritual abstractions become real in the minds of the participants.

There's a general idea that art is somehow separate from life and occurs almost like a religious inspiration. In fact, art is much more like breathing, a kind of taking in and letting go of something invisible yet necessary to life. So when we're out there building a playground, we're creating art, and there may be fifty people out there, and they're all creating art. And everyone goes home with the sense that they created art because they each took responsibility for their own acts.

Building a playground can change people's attitudes about art, what it is, who can create it. Few things are more creative than people planning and building a play structure, not imitating anything around them, but putting their ideas together with their children's visions and making a collective statement that is functional art. This kind of community art has its own aesthetic standards, which reflect a new set of attitudes. Now a pattern of bent-over nails, for example, or an on-the-spot reorganization of the whole structure can be as important artistically as nails that are perfectly straight and flush or plans that are followed exactly.

There's a spiritual quality, too, in this creative process, which comes from people's investing their hard work and their love in a place. And in a way we've come full circle, for that place will pass its spirit of caring on to the children as they play.

Playgrounds are religious places. They're places where special communities of secrets and ritual acts are developed between people. The people may be five years old, but there's still magic and there are still rituals, and they form the basis for an experience which later becomes, if you will, religious. Those experiences need to be protected.

4 What Kind of Structure Do We Want?

This is the nuts-and-bolts part of the book, and the information that follows is intended to put a community group well on the way to completing a play environment. The material here is not simply the reproduction of the blueprints for some existing playgrounds —that would take the fun out of it for you. Instead, the options are identified: the types of frames and their uses, ways to organize whole structures, how to use tools safely and help people work efficiently, and how to put the thing together. Then your group can choose the ideas and construction methods that best suit your needs and the unique environment of your community.

These designs are based on some general criteria, which distinguish them from other kinds of structures. First, the play environments are designed to be built by unskilled workers using easily available tools and

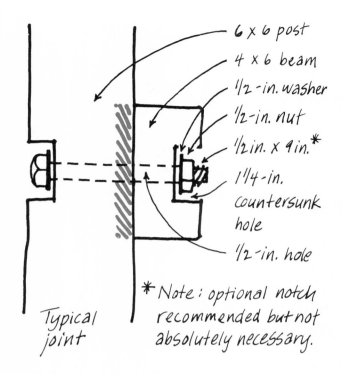

6 x 6 post
4 x 6 beam
1/2-in. washer
1/2-in. nut
1/2 in. x 9 in. *
1 1/4-in. countersunk hole
1/2-in. hole

Typical joint

* Note: optional notch recommended but not absolutely necessary.

materials, so they don't require intricate joints or perfectly square corners, for example. Second, they are planned so that reasonably good carpentry and construction work will result in safe, sturdy structures. And finally, these are play environments, so they don't necessarily have to look like miniature houses or factories or anything else that already exists. Their primary purpose is to provide a relatively safe and diversified environment for play, and if they also happen to look like sculpture, so much the better.

Another important consideration in designing a playground is that the people who use it should be able to see how it works. If the basic structural elements are visible, the playground itself can offer a lesson in design, unlike a house or school building, whose "bones" are hidden behind ceilings and walls.

Building with Wood

Wood is the principal material in most community-built playgrounds for several reasons. The technology of construction with wood is well developed, so a group can engineer a structure by consulting wood-use manuals, usually found in public libraries, for precise information on the strength and distinctive qualities of various woods. The tools and hardware for building with wood also are readily available, and many people have had at least some experience with such equipment. Moreover, wood is amenable to unskilled labor in that it can be shaped or joined without requiring speed or even absolute accuracy. This advantage is particularly apparent when other materials are considered; metal, for instance, is difficult to shape and requires such skills and equipment as those for welding, and cement must be shaped quickly and correctly before it dries.

Wood, too, is the aesthetic preference of many groups, especially in areas where the environment is dominated by metal and concrete. In addition to its intrinsic beauty, wood adds a natural warmth to a space and gives the suggestion of trees if there aren't any living ones there. A wooden structure likewise has a feeling of permanence without seeming to overpower its setting.

CHOICE OF WOOD Since the prices and types of wood available differ from one area to another, it's difficult to suggest

specific kinds of lumber for playground construction. Basically, the lumber in a play structure should be comparable to that used in house framing. The minimum acceptable grade of lumber is standard grade, and select grade is preferable if a group can afford it. When ordering lumber, the group should specify that it be surfaced on four sides. Some people may be reluctant to purchase any new lumber because its use depletes the forests, which is a valid concern. Two alternatives to

buying new lumber are using recycled wood, which often may be purchased from salvage companies, or "found" materials, such as driftwood.

STACKING The simplest way to use lumber for a play structure is to stack it, in much the same way that children build with wooden blocks. The pieces of lumber can then be fastened together easily by drilling holes through them and inserting threaded rod

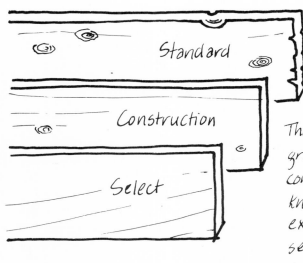

The three grades of lumber used in playground construction are select, which contains only slight defects and few knots; construction, which is less expensive and has more defects than select; and standard, which has many irregularities but is suitable for rough construction.

that is secured at both ends with washers and nuts. Although such structures are simple to build and can be quite attractive, they are also quite expensive because of the massive amounts of lumber they use. This type of construction is often wasteful as well; a "hill" made of lumber stacked on end, for example, does not utilize wood's structural quality, and it offers an experience that is better provided by a mound of dirt.

Many of the wooden play structures sold by commercial equipment manufacturers are based on the stacking principle. These pieces are usually made of high-quality lumber, which is seldom available in local lumberyards. Although such commercially built equipment is relatively expensive, the prices are not out of line for the fine quality of wood with which they are made. When considering purchase of commercial equipment, though, a group must also keep in mind that it will have to pay shipping costs.

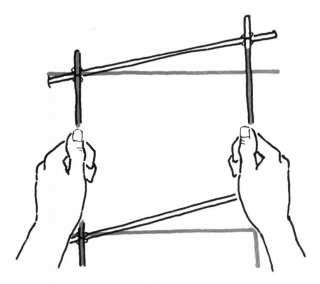

Types of Wood Framing

If the basic design of frames for most structures had to be summarized in one word, it would be "triangle." Almost without exception the triangle is the main structural element in buildings and other forms of construction, even though the structures themselves may be square or rectangular. A pitched (sloping) roof makes a triangle, for instance, and the framing for a rectangular wall usually includes one or more diagonals, which divide the wall into triangles.

A simple model will demonstrate the structural integrity of the triangle and its superiority over a four-sided figure, and this demonstration is also a good way to start kids learning about design. Small, straight pieces of wood and rubber bands will work for this experiment; just make a square with four pieces of wood and a triangle with three pieces, securing them at the corners with the rubber bands. Then test the strength of each structure. When pressure is applied to the triangle, its sides push against each other and so it stays together; but when pressure is applied to one side of the square, it collapses to the opposite side. If diagonals are added down the middle of the square, however, it will no longer fall sideways.

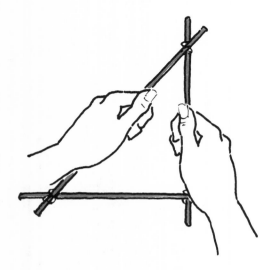

H-FRAME   One exception to the frames that utilize above-ground triangulation is the H, or post-type of construction, which uses the force of the earth for support and rigidity. This is the shape people usually think of first when planning to build with wood because it mirrors the boxlike construction that pre-

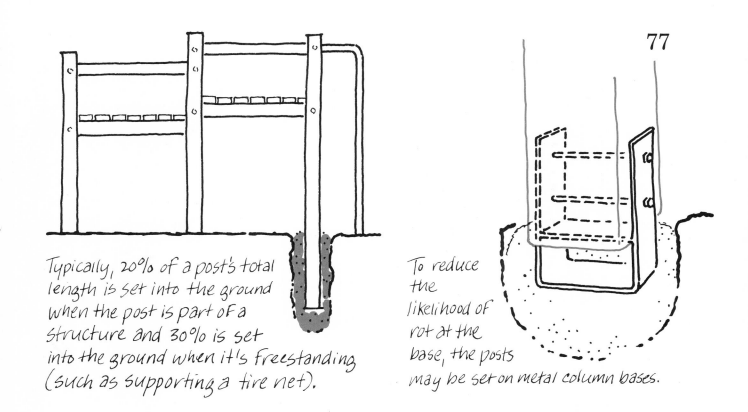

Typically, 20% of a post's total length is set into the ground when the post is part of a structure and 30% is set into the ground when it's freestanding (such as supporting a tire net).

To reduce the likelihood of rot at the base, the posts may be set on metal column bases.

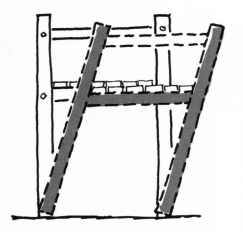

Without concrete footings, a structure lacks stability.

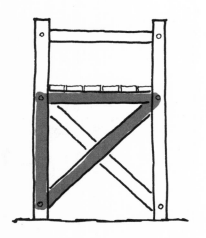

Cross braces make a structure stable.

dominates in our environment. But in order to prevent the H-framework from collapsing, as the four-sided model did, the posts must be set in the ground, which also requires treating the underground portions with preservative and pouring concrete around them. Furthermore, because these buried posts provide invisible support, they don't allow people to see how the structure works, and of course it may be impractical for some groups to dig postholes in their space. But the major disadvantage of H-framing is that since it lacks triangulation, and thus structural integrity, it must be built with heavy lumber, such as 6 × 6-inch posts and 4 × 8-inch beams to support platforms.

The advantages of this type of structure are that the posts can support multiple levels and that private spaces virtually create themselves under the platforms. It's also easy to add safety rails on the side of platforms in H-frames, and the rectilinear shapes have more usable space than some other frame types.

TRIANGULATION   Several kinds of frames can be built to rest directly on the ground by utilizing triangles for support. The H-frame can be made rigid above ground by "flagging," or boards running diagonally between posts. Flagging is both a design and a decorative element in the structure, and it can be used as safety rails or to create areas for privacy.

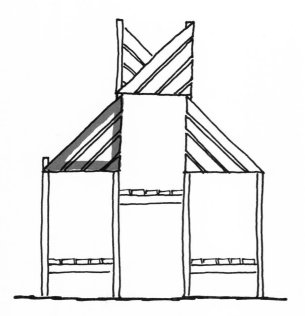

Triangular "Flagging" above platforms.

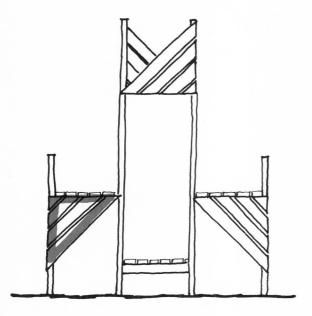

Flagging below platforms.

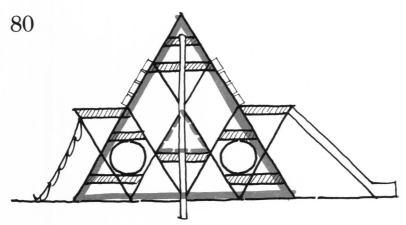

Triangular theme for framework.

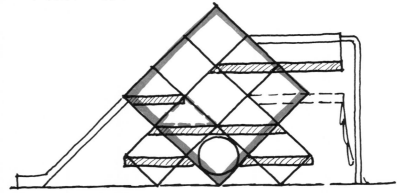

Another possibility: square frame set on end.

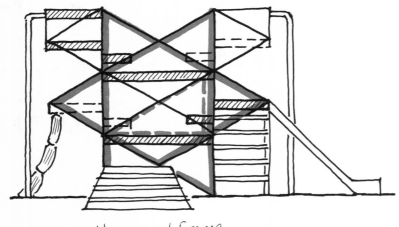

Hexagonal frame.

A-FRAME A-frames make strong and attractive use of the triangle and can be grouped in a variety of ways. They require bracing where platforms are attached, however, and safety rails are rather difficult to install. In addition, the A-frame limits usable space above the platform, necessitating careful planning for head room.

One way to use the A-frame is as a substitute for posts. This type of A-framing gives a structure a vertical, soaring quality through its use of rather tall, A-shaped towers (see illustration). The spatial organization with these towers is similar to that of an H-frame

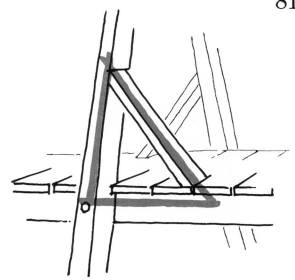

Triangular bracing of A-frame.

A-frame playground with parachute canopy.

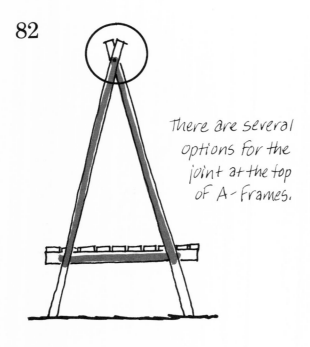

There are several options for the joint at the top of A-frames.

structure, but the A-frames rest on top of the ground, rather than being set into it. As with vertical H-frames, though, the towerlike A-frames must be built with massive lumber to be stable.

Another type of A-framing uses medium-sized lumber. In this denser pattern of A's, which one group called the "teahouse" design, the A-motif establishes the visual and environmental quality of a space, rather than being an isolated structural element (see illustration). The teahouse design also offers a good means of creating areas for kids' privacy or shelter from bad weather.

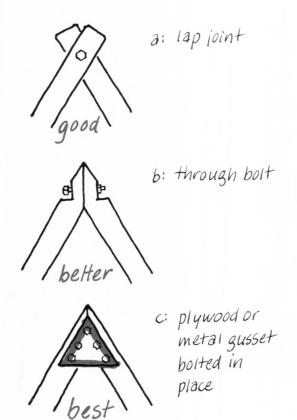

a: lap joint

good

b: through bolt

better

c: plywood or metal gusset bolted in place

best

Steps in construction of A-frame "teahouse" design. Step 1: Preassembling of A-frame.

Step 2: A-frames tipped up and connected in series by beams.

Step 3: Attachment of flooring.

Step 4: Installation of ridgepole.

Step 5: Installation of stairs, ramps, and auxiliary decks.

Finished structure.

W-FRAME The W-frame is another design that achieves triangulation with square lumber. This framing system utilizes three triangles, two of which are upside down, thus giving a central A-shape with "wings" on both sides. One advantage of the W- over the A-frame is that platforms can be attached at different heights, whereas the A-frame tends to create long platforms or corridors at one level. Moreover, four W-frames can be joined at the tips of the wings to form a square structure. This arrangement employs triangulation while requiring only simple joints and 90° angles, which makes construction relatively quick and easy. An additional site for attachment of a platform is where the corners of two W's meet, so four levels of platforms can be created on one side of the W-frame square. The W-frame also facilitates use of guardrails, which can be attached to the wing tips that extend above platforms.

Both the W- and A-frames are two-dimensional and therefore require bracing to keep from falling over. In the towerlike A-frame structure, the bracing is attached to platforms, while in W-frames the braces run diagonally from the top center of the frame to the ground, like a sort of outrigger (see illustration). Diagonal braces can also serve as support for an interior platform in the square that is formed by joining four W-frames.

Steps in construction of W-frame. Step 1: W-frame laid out on site. Triangles created by W-frame are equilateral.

Step 2: Angles for joints have been cut at 30°, holes drilled, and threaded rod inserted and bolted into place. Step 3: Installation of safety rail and top-level support beam for platform.

Step 4: W-frame being tilted up.

Step 5: Attachment of W-frame "outrigger" support brace and platform support.

Step 6: Attachment of interior brace and platform onto W-frame. Note that W-frames have been joined to form the sides of a square.

Detail of corner; note metal corner brace at platform joint.

Step 7: Installation of supports for third-level platform; note short 4 x 4 in corner.

Step 8: Installation of support for decking for third- and fourth-level platforms.

Step 9: 2 x 6 decking in place on all platform levels.

Top view showing tires in center space.

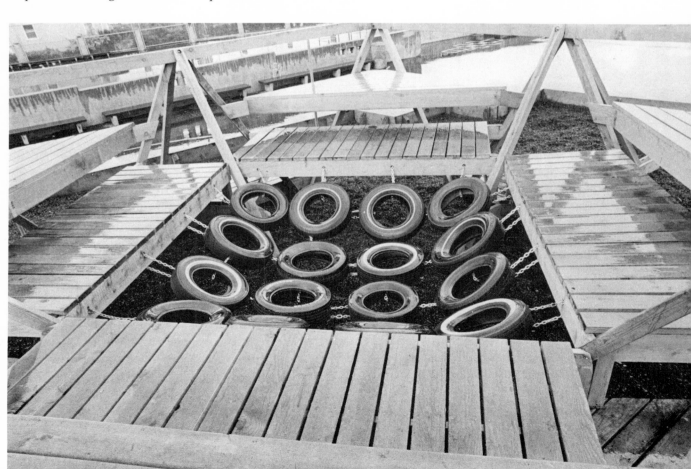

Outrigger support and platform at upper end of X-frame.

X-FRAME   Yet another type of frame that utilizes triangulation is the X, which might also be called an overlapping A-frame. When joined together in a series, these X's form a spine to which platforms and play equipment can be attached. Like the W- and A-frames, the X-frame needs side braces, and in this design each brace can support one side of a platform.

The X-frame is particularly well suited to a structure that will be used by children of varying size and age, since the platforms can be placed at many different heights. One group, for instance, made one end of a structure with low platforms and equipment, and progressively increased the height, and thus the difficulty, by making larger X's at the other end of the spine. The X-frame also takes advantage of simple joints with square lumber, as the platforms attach to the braces at a 90° angle.

In addition to their unusually attractive appearance, these more sophisticated designs, such as the teahouse, W-, and X-frames, allow maximum use of space and require only medium-sized lumber, such as 4 × 4s for framing and 2 × 6s for decking. Because lumber costs proportionally more per board foot in larger dimensions (such as 6 × 6) and there are more board feet in a 6 × 6 than in a 4 × 4 of equal length, a structure built of medium-sized wood could cost 50 per cent less than a comparable one of heavy lumber, even though there may be more individual pieces of the smaller lumber.

X-frame structure gets progressively higher from one end to the other.

Installation of safety rails requires ingenuity.

Varied traffic corridor through X-frames.

LOGS Round elements can add a new dimension to the designing of structures, and logs often have advantages over straight-sided lumber. First, logs may be much less expensive than lumber, especially if they are left over from some other process. Second, unlike square lumber, they are adaptable to designs in which the pieces join at odd angles, since their surfaces meet in the same way no matter what the angle. Finally, the round elements always have a surface that kids can handle, which is not the case with square lumber when it is turned at an angle exposing its edge.

In addition to being support elements, logs make fine climbing structures in themselves. Children play differently on a log structure than on one of multilevel platforms; they tend to keep three points of contact with the structure and to move slowly and carefully on it. So this type of environment offers an experience not found in other types of framing because of its treelike nature; instead of playing a fast game of tag, for instance, kids will go there to get away from the frantic activity and just perch atop the logs to watch for a while.

Two uncommon types of structure can be built with logs such as peeler cores (the round, eight-foot-long remnants of plywood production), telephone poles, or tree trunks. A climbing structure of logs, for example, can be used in conjunction with other structures on a playground, or as the main event. One thing to keep in mind about logs is that when they are available, they're generally cheaper than regular lumber. This may be especially true of telephone poles or

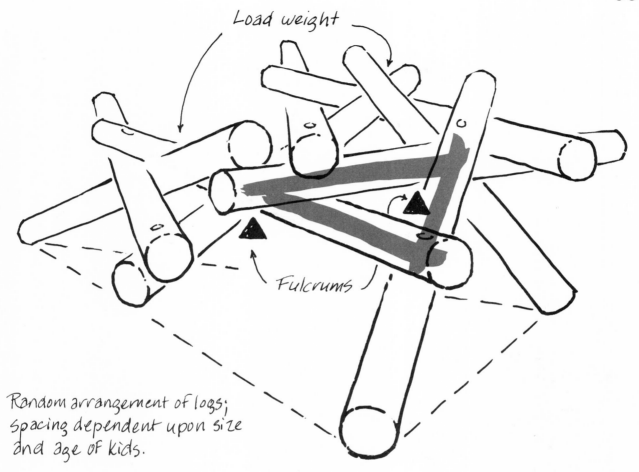

Load weight

Fulcrums

Random arrangement of logs;
spacing dependent upon size
and age of kids.

tree trunks, if a good source of them can be found. Whatever wood is used should be smooth, at least on the surfaces where children will be climbing.

One type of construction with logs is a random arrangement, which encourages much on-site designing of the structure. An aesthetically interesting and challenging way to build with these round pieces is to try to have as few points as possible on the ground; for example, there could be ten or fifteen logs in the air and only three points of contact with the ground. This arrangement gives a

feeling of lightness to the structure and permits a lot of movement through the space, both on the ground and above it.

The random design still is based on triangles, although their angles and sizes vary considerably within the structure. An efficient method of attachment is with threaded rod and nuts (as explained in the following discussion of the running-man design). The one tricky part of this random arrangement is wedging the ends of logs among several others to provide adequate support for the whole structure. This requires

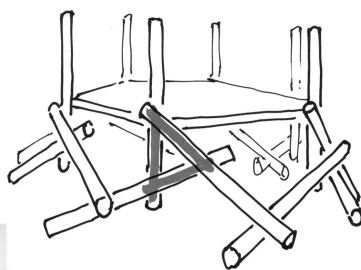

Running men in orderly arrangement.

some experimenting before fastening pieces together and some patient people to hold all the pieces in place until the structure can stand by itself.

A second log design is similar to an Indian motif called the running man, a sort of off-center A-frame arrangement. This design offers a more regular appearance and yields a more organized structure than the random design, and its individual frames can be built as units and then assembled. Because the logs overlap in the running-man design, each unit has six ends that extend beyond the joints where the logs are bolted together. These extensions allow the frames to be readily arranged into large, rather loose structures, again utilizing the wedging technique for connecting units.

A running-man structure is most easily built by two work crews. The first crew makes the running-man units, in the following

steps: (1) laying out the logs in the overlapping triangle form; (2) one person holding and one countersinking (drilling a short, wide hole so that the nut and bolt are below the log's surface); (3) one person drilling a long hole through the logs; (4) then the second person countersinking the back side of each log; (5) two people putting threaded rods through the holes in the logs, adding a washer and nut at each end, and tightening them with a socket wrench. The second crew assembles the individual units, wedging and bolting them together in an arrangement that allows movement through the space and accommodates any apparatus to be added to the structure. This crew will have to support the units until three or four frames are wedged one in another, and then it will stand alone.

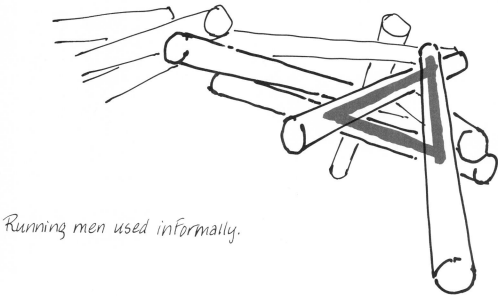

Running men used informally.

TRUNCATED TETRAHEDRON

Square lumber can also be used for an angled climbing structure that is similar to one made of logs, but the difficulty is the complex joints required to fit lumber together at odd angles. One solution to this problem is a tetrahedron, which is a sort of three-dimensional triangle. This type of structure offers a climbing environment that is halfway between a rock and a tree, since a child uses her whole body to move on the surface of a tetrahedron, rather than stepping from place to place or pulling herself from one level to another with just her arms.

This tetrahedron design is truncated, meaning that its ends have been cut off, and it is regular, meaning that its sides are all the same length. It consists of six side pieces, which can be railroad ties or 4 × 6 lumber,

and four end pieces, which are exterior-grade, 1-inch plywood. Truncation requires that the ends of all side pieces be cut at a predetermined angle (55°); the size of the end pieces depends on the dimensions of the lumber used. The angle of truncation is the same whatever the size of the tetrahedron, but its sides must always be of equal length (or the angles are extremely difficult to determine).

These structures are easy to build and can be used in groups. Plywood "skins" also can be added to the sides, either by direct attachment or with rope lacing, to create closed spaces or shaded areas. The truncated tetrahedron also is movable; by lifting it at the bottom corner, the structure can be rolled to an alternate side with moderate effort. Thus, small tetrahedrons could serve as portable equipment in fenced playgrounds or other areas where the units can't be rolled away.

Truncated tetrahedron: make six legs
cut at 55° and four 1-inch exterior
plywood end
plates.

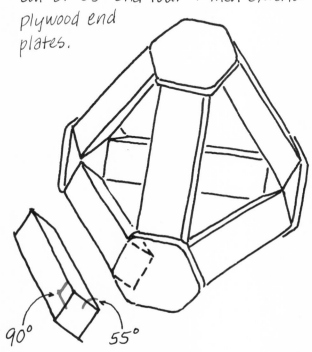

90°   55°

POLYHEDRON HILL   A similar type of design is utilized in the polyhedron hill, an assemblage of many-sided figures in a large, intricate structure. Children play differently on this honeycomblike structure than on a tetrahedron, as they move both inside it and on its surfaces. A polyhedron hill can offer many of the experiences that an entire playground includes because it accommodates privacy and quiet play, as well as climbing and active play in its open spaces. This structure has a trim, modern appearance that is an asset to any environment.

A polyhedron hill should be constructed of hard-skinned, heavy-density overlay plywood, as should any outdoor structure that calls for plywood. The playground pictured here is the work of architectural designer David Gast. One unusual feature of this structure is that it can be disassembled and moved from one place to another. Polyhedron structures also can be used indoors for play, or as individual learning spaces. They are available from commercial manufacturers, and sources of design information for polyhedrons are listed in the bibliography.

Polyhedron hill, designed by David Gast of the Community Design Center, San Francisco.

Third beam being added to tripod; note unit laid out on ground and completed tripod (at left).

TRIPODS   The tripod frame is a three-dimensional triangular form, similar to a tetrahedron. The lumber's flat surfaces fit squarely together, however, and its three members cross each other and extend both up and down from that junction. This design is extremely strong, its members rest on the ground, and it has a minimum of clutter around the platforms and other play equipment. In addition, a group of tripods can make a large, graceful play structure appropriate in scale for a sizable space, such as a meadow, where a smaller form might seem to be swallowed up.

If not held together by horizontal braces, the three main tripod beams will fall down in a rather curious circular unfolding. Braces can be added above or below the junction of the beams, but since long braces are more effective than short ones, they are generally put above the junction, where the ends of beams are farther apart. When one of the tripods stands alone, its hourglass shape makes the upper portion flexible. The junction of the tripod acts rather like a person's waist, permitting flexible movement of the upper body while the lower portion is relatively still. Because this flexibility can cause fatigue at the tripod's central junction, these units are usually built in a series of three or more, rather than as single structures, for purposes of stability.

Central joint of tripod.

Tie braces being installed; these become platform supports.

Decking being installed; note "anchors" (center), which provide cantilever support for tire swings.

Railings and equipment installed.

CANTILEVERS All of the frame types described here can be used to support cantilevered parts. A cantilever is a balance system in which a weight that acts on an arm projecting from a rigid support is counterbalanced by a pull in the opposite direction on the opposite side. The action around the fulcrum contained in the support is called the moment of force. The weight on the fulcrum can be equalized by a tension element or a compression element (see illustration). A cantilever does put additional stress on the beams supporting it, so these beams between posts must be of a larger dimension than if not used as cantilevers; for instance, 4 × 8 beams would be needed where 2 × 8 lumber would otherwise be sufficient.

The frame of a wooden structure can

provide the rigid support for a cantilever, and in fact some portion of the platforms on most play structures are cantilevered. This feature is easy to recognize, since a part of the structure extends beyond the posts to which it is attached so that the platform seems to be unsupported on one side. One important advantage of cantilevered platforms is the safety element they provide; if a child falls off an extended platform, for example, he won't land on structural framework. Cantilevered areas also increase the amount of play surface and give the children an open, outward orientation, since the framing members are not the outer limits of the structure.

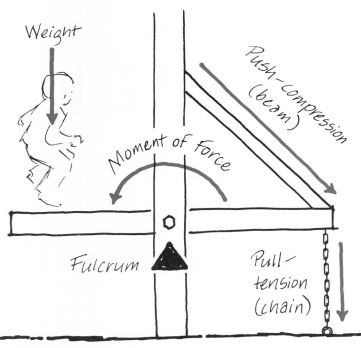

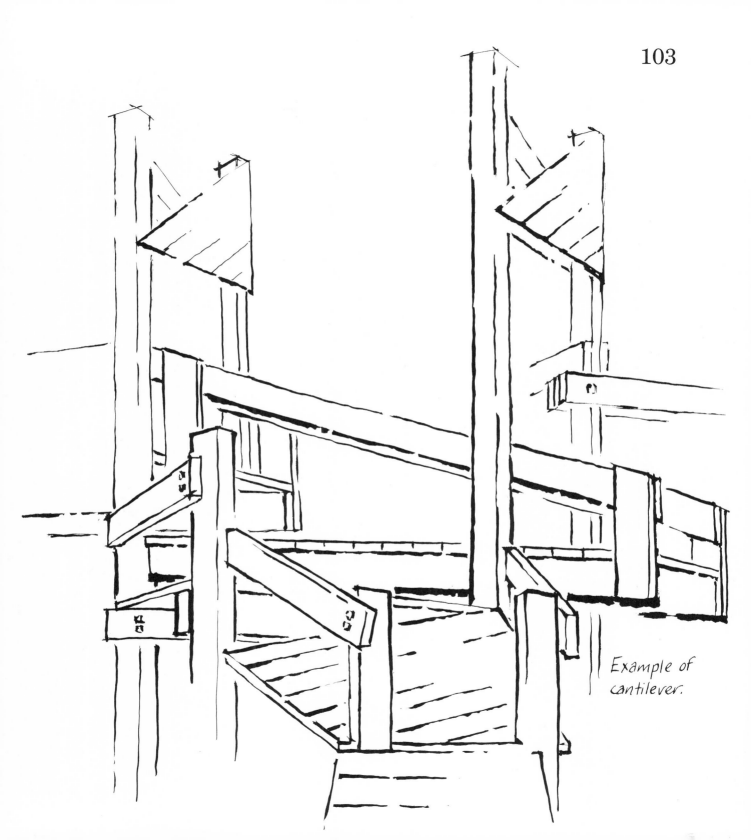

Example of cantilever.

Organization of Structures

The type of framing is one choice to be made in planning an active-play environment; another is the organization of those frames into a finished structure. Both of these decisions are influenced by the size and shape of the space where they will be built. If a schoolyard is long and narrow, for instance, a large, circular tripod structure isn't going to fit.

The way kids use a play space is also a consideration for organizing a structure. An active-play structure could be described as a sort of staircase, a corridor of movement that has various events along it. A child moving through such a space is using her whole body vigorously, jumping, dodging, crawling quickly, and balancing while in motion.

Ideally a group should aim to create a structure that uses both its resources and the available space as efficiently as possible while offering a variety of play experiences for the children. Several ways to achieve this objective are discussed here in order of increasing complexity.

LINEAL PROGRESSION   The most fundamental way of organizing play equipment is in a straight line. This arrangement creates a straightforward means of integrating equipment within a single pattern of movement. A lineal structure can become a sort of obstacle course, with the disadvantage that it doesn't promote flow within the space or social interaction. Kids are programmed by the structure's layout and have little choice but to go straight through the apparatus, get off, and go back to the start. This repetition gets old in a hurry, and it restricts the diversity of experience and interaction children might enjoy if the same equipment were arranged differently.

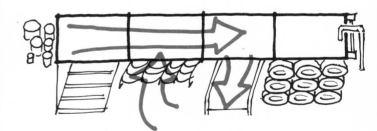

Lineal progression creates an obstacle course.

Without making the structure more difficult to build, a group could enhance social interaction by putting two short lineal structures side by side, then filling the space between them with other activities. This more concentrated arrangement begins to "recycle" the kids, and the physical dynamic of their environment fosters their playing

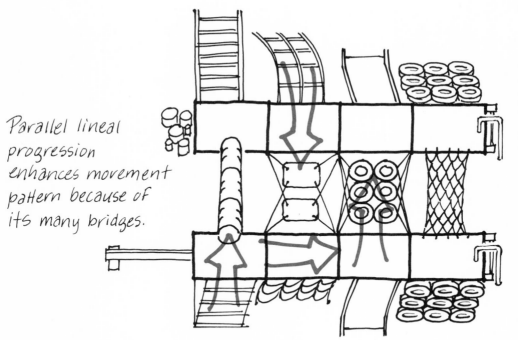

Parallel lineal progression enhances movement pattern because of its many bridges.

Zigzag platforms.

with each other, rather than just moving down a long line of equipment.

Another way to improve an essentially lineal arrangement is to make it accordion shaped, or zigzagged. This modification permits kids to go down the slide, for instance, and then choose to go on or return to the slide, without being swept along with the single straight line of traffic in a lineal space. Although the individual pieces of equipment are somewhat less accessible in a zigzag structure, the loss is offset by the increased spatial interest of this arrangement; that is, compressing the structure creates odd-shaped spaces and private areas not found in a long, narrow avenue. Another type of zigzag arrangement that incorporates both spatial interest and continuity of movement is two Z-shaped structures facing each other (see illustration). This double-Z structure is also more readily adapted to a confined space than most other lineal forms.

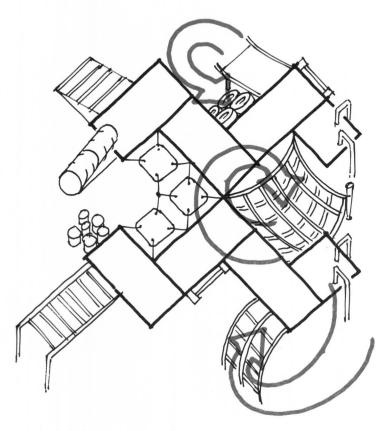

Zigzag layout creates small loops of movement.

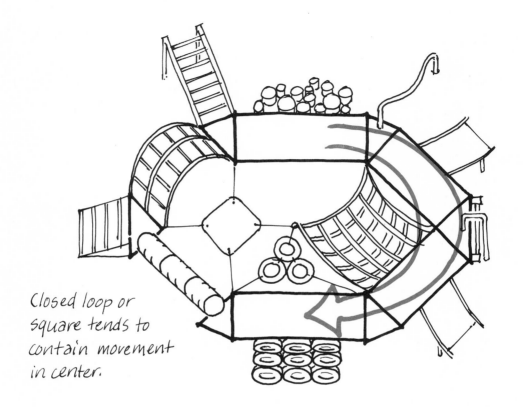

Closed loop or
square tends to
contain movement
in center.

LOOP   A significant improvement on the lineal organization is arrangement of the equipment in a loop or closed pattern, such as a circular or square structure. This allows kids the choice of moving outward (down a fire pole, say), inward (into a cargo net), or on around the structure. And of course the levels of platforms can be varied in any type of structure to create a maximum of play opportunities in the space.

SPIRAL   Limited space can be used even more efficiently by a spiral arrangement of platforms, built on the same principle as a spiral staircase. For example, around a central point there could be a 2-foot platform, beside it a 4-foot one, a 6-foot one beside that, and finally an 8-foot platform directly above the 2-foot one. Spirals can be built adjacent to one another to provide even more choices of activity. This type of design also reduces the amount of material needed, since one post can support a corner of four platforms. More important, the spiral arrangement is appropriate to the way children like to use the playground, creating focal points for their convoluted, almost furious movement, yet allowing free flow from one area to another.

Double-spiral ascending platforms.

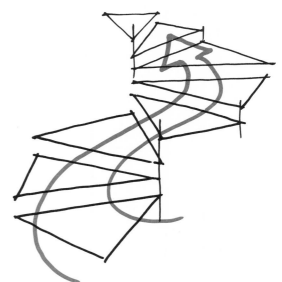

Ascending double spiral.

OVERLAPPING   All types of frames can be arranged so that one platform overlaps another, as in the spiral design. In addition to utilizing space well, overlapping can create private, sheltered areas, which may be especially desirable in places that are often windy or foggy. In a structure with more complex use of overlapping, several corridors of movement can intersect; such a structure offers many alternatives for activities and accommodates large numbers of children at one time.

Lineal progression from lower to higher makes each platform the right height for equipment.

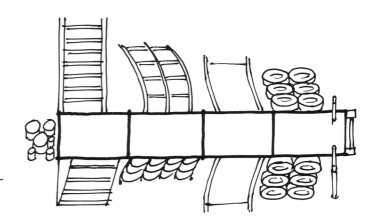

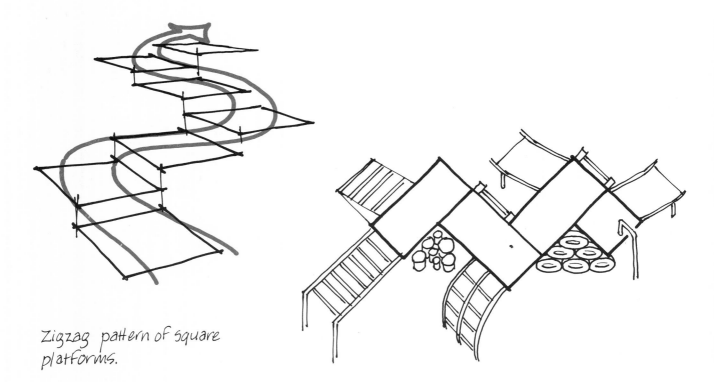

Zigzag pattern of square platforms.

Zigzag pattern of triangular platforms.

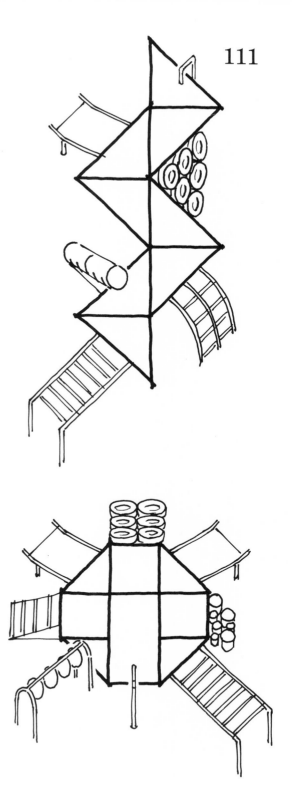

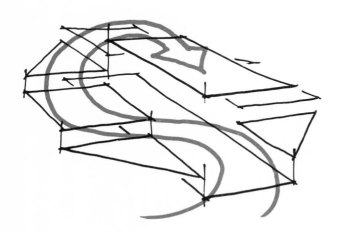

Multilevel octagon with highest level directly over lowest.

Even without an intellectual analysis of space, a group probably would arrive at a design that includes overlapping areas and complex intersections because people intuitively understand that such a structure is best suited to the flow of children's energy and movement when playing. The discussion of design and organization in the preceding pages has gone from the simplest lineal structure to the most complex, and hence advantageous, type of structure to provide an overview of planning possibilities. A group's members should try to build the most complex structure they can realistically accomplish, but if compromises are necessary, they can fall back to a slightly less ambitious structure instead of reverting to the simplest form possible.

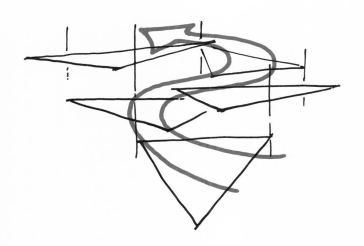

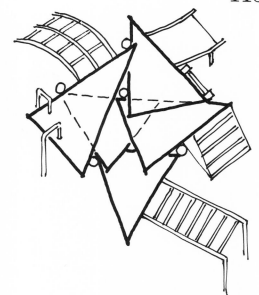

Overlapping triangles (see cantilever).

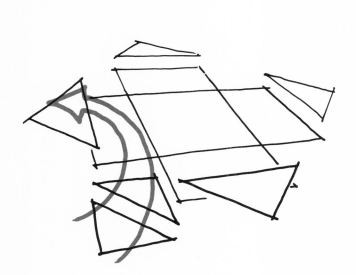

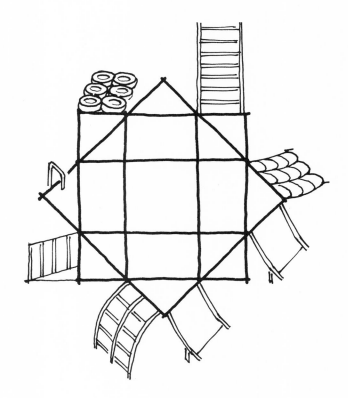

Design based on a quilting pattern called
"The Children of Israel" (see W-frame).

Discovering a Theme

Another approach to planning a play environment is to select a theme and let it generate the actual design. The theme could be an idea, a shape, a pattern, an object, or anything that interests the group. Members of a religious organization, for instance, might choose a symbol that has particular meaning to them and use it as an organizing theme. Others might make the rule that no vertical lines could be used in the framework of their structure, or they may decide to use certain materials only in their natural forms, such as tree trunks instead of lumber.

This seemingly arbitrary way of designing offers a different challenge to a group than planning according to activities. Instead of designing a structure to accommodate anticipated behavior of children, the group decides on a specific shape that determines the character of environment and creates enough complexity to absorb the children's energy. Such a design process often combines a strong aesthetic statement with great potential for variety of experience and for inventiveness in the use of the theme.

SUFI MAGIC SQUARE   One example of thematic design for a play structure is the use of the Sufi magic square. The method of creating shapes by connecting numbers on this chart articulates space according to an ancient, mystical tradition that has seldom been used in Western societies. A few minutes of experimentation with the Sufi square will yield many interesting shapes that you'd never think of otherwise, and building a structure based on these forms could be rewarding as well as challenging.

MANDALA   Another possible design inspiration is the mandala, which offers visually exciting ways of looking at patterns in space. A mandala design could be based on quilting patterns, for instance, or it might be an intricate, multiple mirror image of one geometric shape. These symmetrical forms are efficient, too, because the repetition of shape permits an almost assembly-line method of construction. A mandala structure creates an environment that is ordered and has a tailored appearance, yet it contrasts effectively with the boxlike architecture that predominates in the environment.

Sufi magic square with design.

5 What Play Experiences Should We Have?

The type of frame and its organization into a structure are important considerations in playground planning, and selection of the play experiences to be included in the environment is equally important. A really complete environment should provide for the three principal types of play, that is, active, climbing, and quiet play, as well as offering such related activities as an art table, workbench, and nature area. Although most community groups can't afford such a comprehensive play area all at once, it is important that all of these elements be included in a group's long-term planning.

The first phase of building should always include an active-play center, which can also provide areas for climbing and quiet play. Because diversity and choice of activity are major objectives in such a play center, a good rule is to make each thing unique on the playground. This may seem difficult because there are only a few basic types of equipment, such as swings, slides, and climbers, but these may be varied by changing the way they are used and the size, scale, materials, or texture each time that piece of equipment is built into a structure. A ladder, for instance, could be vertical, horizontal, or on a slant, and it might be made of wood, metal, rope, chain, or tires.

Equipment for Active Play

A child engaged in active play is using his whole body, moving rapidly through a space and testing and developing skill, strength, balance, coordination, and bodily awareness. Active play includes fast games such as kickball, basketball, or tag, as well as play on such equipment as swings, slides, or fire poles. Except for swings, which must be somewhat segregated for safety, the equipment for active play can be arranged in a structure that has platforms as stations for access to these activities. By integrating such equipment into a structure, the activities become features in a landscape, rather than isolated events. Thus, a game of chase can move up a ladder, through several levels of platforms, and down a slide, instead of happening mostly on a flat, hard surface. And though this frantic activity may look chaotic, the children are moving through this space in a pattern that is responsive to the movements of other children.

In addition, an active-play structure helps protect the whole space around it by becoming the focus of kids' energies, so they don't have only the trees and bushes to play in, for example. And even if only a small percentage of children are using the structure at a given moment, its presence alleviates the competitive, antisocial pressure kids feel when there is nothing to do in a play space.

WIDE SLIDE   The wide slide tends to be a focus of activity on the playground, and many games take place around it. The up-and-down movements facilitated by a wide slide are fundamental parts of active play, although to avoid collisions it is wise to minimize the amount of movement in both directions on the same slide. This might be accomplished by having two slides, one up and one down, or putting similar up-and-down activities, such as a fire pole and an interesting ladder, on either side of the slide.

Regardless of the ground cover used on the playground, rubber matting should be installed at the foot of the slide to absorb the impact of kids as they come down the slick metal surface. If loose material such as sand or tanbark is used, the rubber still is needed underneath it, since this type of ground cover will be quickly pushed away from the base of the slide.

The run-off at the end of the slide is a source of some debate among playground designers. A child has a more abrupt impact at the end of a slide that goes straight to the ground than on one with a "lip" at the end. But if the lip is more than a few inches off the

ground, the child might go sailing off and land in a sitting position, which could cause injury to the coccyx (tailbone). The safest alternative, then, is a slide that ends with a lip from which the drop is no more than 6 inches.

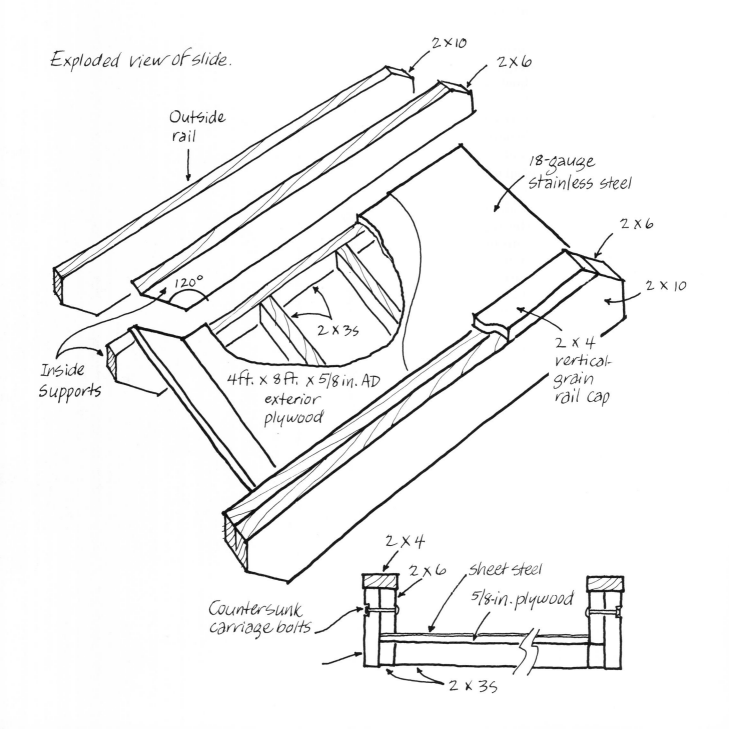

Exploded view of slide.

2×10

2×6

Outside rail

18-gauge stainless steel

2×6

2×10

120°

2×3s

2×4 vertical-grain rail cap

Inside Supports

4ft. × 8ft. × 5/8 in. AD exterior plywood

2×4

2×6

sheet steel

5/8-in. plywood

Countersunk carriage bolts

2×3s

*There's more than one way
to come down a fire pole.*

FIRE POLE   A fire pole isn't just an exit;
it's a great exit, particularly for getting out of
real or imaginary scrapes. The fire pole must
be placed so that the kids coming down it are
not in a traffic pattern for other activities,
and rubber should be installed at the bottom
of the pole, since any loose ground cover will
be pushed away by the children's feet. If the
pole is attached to a platform that has a
second platform underneath it, the lower one
should be walled off so that someone coming
off that platform can't collide with a person
coming down the fire pole.

INCLINED SLIDING POLE   A varia-
tion on the fire pole is the inclined sliding
pole, which is a sort of metal banister. This
pole also can be curved, and it provides
another fine exit from a platform.

Spinning opens new channels between the cerebral cortices.

TURNING BARS   Turning bars are an important part of the active-play structure because children develop and refine their coordination on them. The kids make up tricks and movements for this equipment that require great agility and strength, and when they've mastered one set of movements they develop even more challenging ones. Because turning bars can be somewhat dangerous, rubber matting should be placed beneath them to cushion a child's fall if she misses a trick.

BALANCE BEAM   Balance beams can easily be built into an active-play structure as avenues from one activity to another. This experience is basic to physical poise, and it can be varied by tapering the balance beam, making it incline slightly, or changing its surface by using round material.

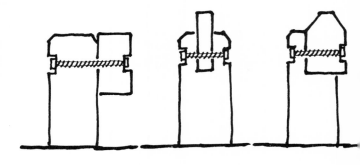

Several construction methods for balance beams.

Balance beam for free play or physical education.

RAMPS   Ramps provide yet another way to get on or off a play structure, and they help children develop eye-foot coordination. The surface texture of a ramp can be varied to prevent its getting slippery, or a small gap can be left between boards for a somewhat different experience. Some children may be reluctant to walk on such an open ramp, for fear of falling through, just as some adults are nervous about walking or sitting on open bleachers. The urge to play and the obviously safe passage of other children will help kids overcome this fear, however. Like balance beams, ramps can be varied in shape; for example, they might be curvilinear or wide in the middle and narrow at both ends.

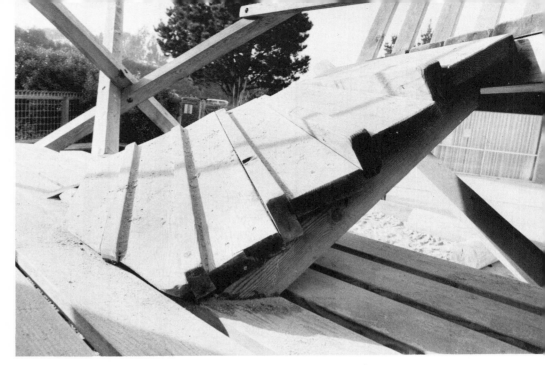

Ramps can have irregular surfaces.

Pipe-ladder ramp.

LADDERS In general, ladders are overused in play structures. The climbing experience should be different each time it is repeated on the playground, and there are many ways to vary it. A ladder can be made of wood, metal, rope, chain, or tires, and the size and scale can be changed with each material used.

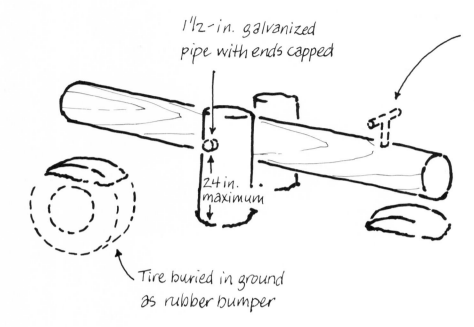

1½-in. galvanized pipe with ends capped

24 in. maximum

Tire buried in ground as rubber bumper

Note: Do not put on a handle. It is potentially damaging to teeth and lack of handle makes for stronger legs and a challenging balance beam.

HORIZONTAL LADDER   The skill that kids develop on the horizontal ladder is called brachiation, and it is one of a very few experiences that are new to children on the playground, since they don't begin to do this movement until age five or six. Kids also like to walk across the top of the ladder, on the rungs or on the sides, so the horizontal ladder should be as low as possible while still allowing the tallest child to hang by his hands without touching the ground. For elementary-school-age children, the maximum height is about 7½ feet. The ladder should also be wide enough to permit two children to cross on top and two to cross hand over hand at the same time; a good width for this purpose is 4 feet.

One potential hazard on the horizontal ladder is in mounting and dismounting. To prevent a child from falling onto the vertical steps up to the ladder, the first rung at each end of the horizontal part should be set in, rather than directly above the steps. This also gets the child in a good position to begin the hand-over-hand movement, since he must lean forward to reach the first rung.

The rungs of a horizontal ladder usually are made of galvanized pipe, since solid metal bars are hard to find. On a 4-foot-wide ladder, this pipe must be 1¼ inches in diameter; anything smaller will bend from the weight of the older children swinging on it. Most kids can't close their hands over these rather large rungs, but this unusual way of grasping the bars develops the muscles of the forearm, which are not utilized much in other playground activities.

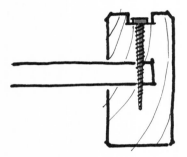

Attach bar with lag screw.

Raising top step and recessing first rung corrects this awkward dismounting problem.

Rung of horizontal ladder made with 1 1/4-inch pipe.

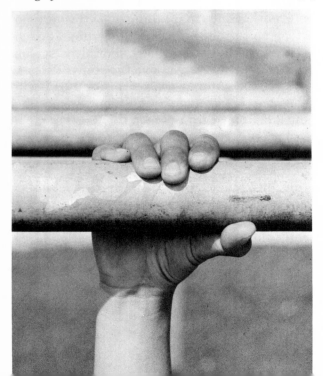

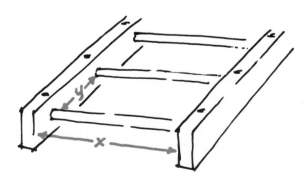

For kids under six years old, distance X is 30 to 36 inches and y is 12 to 14 inches. Pipe size is 1-inch inside diameter. For over six, X is 40 to 48 inches. Y is 14 to 18 inches and pipe is 1 1/4-inch diameter.

SIZE AND AGE RANGES FOR USE OF PLAY EQUIPMENT.

A	Horizontal ladder	5 ft. high
B	Bar spacing	12 in. apart
C	Crawl space	20 in. high and wide
D	Step height	12 in. high
E	Safety-rail height	34 in. deck to top of rail
F	Fire-pole reach	16 in. out

For the average 6-year-old. Make equipment 10% larger per added year of age.

Equipment \ Age	0-1	1-2	2-3	3-4	5-6	7-8-9	10-13	14-up
Slide		■	■	■	■	■	■	■
Fire pole			■	■	■	■	■	■
Turning bar			■	■	■	■	■	■
Balance beam		■	■	■	■	■	■	
Ramp	■	■	■	■	■	■	■	
Horizontal ladder			■	■	■	■	■	■
Chain / rope ladder			■	■	■	■	■	■
Tunnel		■	■	■	■	■		■
Suspended platform			■	■	■	■	■	■
Arch or dome climber			■	■	■	■	■	■
Swing		■	■	■	■	■	■	■
Treelike climber			■	■	■	■	■	■
Net with rope			■	■		■	■	■
Private area		■	■	■	■	■	■	

RING SET   Another device for brachiation is a ring set, which adds the experience of a movable ring to the pendulum motion of the body. This equipment is available inexpensively from commercial manufacturers.

swing goes up and out of sight, it's coming right back down. Swinging gives kids some pectoral muscle development, and it's a sensation they love—they're flying. The best possible swing is a rope tied to a tree limb, on which kids can soar out over a pond, but this kind of swing is too dangerous for any high-density area like a park or playground.

Any type of swing requires massive, rigid, permanent framework to support the weight and inertia of children. The frame itself can be dangerous, too, since it is usually the highest point on a playground and some kids will always try to climb it. The swing bearings are the most important part of the apparatus. A swing must have heavy-duty (expensive) bearings made of tempered steel; any other type of bearing will wear out quickly. This is the greatest potential hazard of a swing because if the bearing fails, this massive chunk of metal may fall right on the head of a child in the swing. So in addition to using only the strongest bearings available, they should be inspected and lubricated periodically to insure their safe operation.

SWINGS Swings are by far the most controversial element of a playground because they are what kids always want first, but they're expensive and provide a source of activity for only a small number of children. Many people consider any kind of swing dangerous, and the conventional swing set definitely can be a hazard to very young children, who don't realize that when the

Three-fourths-inch eye bolt worn through after two weeks of use on a tire swing.

TIRE SWING   The best all-around solution to the problems inherent in all swings is the tire swing. Several kids can use it at once, and it has a circular motion instead of the conventional back-and-forth action. Because the tire swing has a smaller range of motion than other swings, it has less danger of collision than a swing that disappears from view and then comes flying back.

A tire swing requires a special type of bearing because of its circular motion. Only a universal joint or a ball joint will serve this purpose, and a swivel must be used with the universal joint to prevent the chains from winding up as the swing revolves.

Like any other kind of swing, the tire swing should be placed out of the traffic flow on the playground and should have ample clearance from any part of the structure. If there is a possibility that the swing might hit some part of its framework, the swing's action can be reduced with a chain, one end of which is

Homemade swing joint: bolt connected to an automobile drive shaft and a swivel.

attached to the bottom of the swing, with the other end attached to a swivel that has been set in concrete in the ground. The swivel can be placed away from the center of the tire swing so that kids are less likely to step or fall on it when getting on and off the swing.

COMMERCIAL EQUIPMENT   The various kinds of commercial equipment found in the typical city-built playground are not included here because the safety record for these pieces of equipment is just too poor. Such apparatus as a merry-go-round or a metal trapeze is too dangerous to be worth the risk or the money it would cost a community to buy and install it.

Tire-swing frame that uses cable as tension element for support.

A chain-link climber.

Equipment for Climbing Play

Climbing play is slower and more tactile than active play. Kids use their hands and arms for traction, pulling themselves along or over parts of a structure, rather than throwing their bodies through space. Climbing activity is basic to development of gross motor skills, particularly body control and coordination of the hands and feet for balance on uneven, changing surfaces. A great variety of climbing experiences can be offered on the playground by utilizing both rigid surfaces, such as rocks or trees, and flexible ones, such as ropes or tires.

TREES   One way to provide the tree-climbing experience for kids on a playground is by setting sound, dead trees in the ground with cement. These trees, which usually consist of the trunk and several large branches, are often available from city maintenance yards, highway departments, or building contractors, any of whom may be cutting down healthy trees in preparation for new projects. For playground use trees should be hardwood, if available, and have no rot or termites. Besides being natural climbers, such trees retain the structural integrity of wood and are intrinsically stronger than anything made of boards held together with nuts and bolts. Use of partial trees in a play structure requires flexibility of design and on-site experimentation, which often results in an ingenious and highly unusual playground.

Built to kids' code.

One disadvantage of using trees is that as they get older, a limb can break off under the kids' weight. This danger can be minimized by attaching the trees together so that if a limb gives way, it will still be supported by another tree or limb and won't come crashing down. Portions of trees can also be turned upside-down or laid sideways to allow children to climb without being so far off the ground.

Other wooden climbing structures can be made with logs, such as the random arrangement and the running-man design, or with straight-sided lumber, such as the tetrahedron made of railroad ties.

METAL TREES   Treelike climbing devices can also be made of metal. They are especially good for high-density play areas, where use is constant and maintenance is minimal. Such a climber is the welded-steel tree, which might be created with surplus automobile exhaust pipes or other salvage metal. Its design goal should be to make the climbing challenge lateral instead of vertical. Certain commerical equipment likewise duplicates the tree-climbing experience. Such metal devices as the cube climber and jungle gym are popular playground items, but these pieces have the significant fault that if a child falls from the top, he'll sort of ricochet off the bars beneath him. Two commercial climbers that do not have this built-in hazard are the arch climber and the geodesic dome.

ROCKS Another natural climbing experience is offered by large rocks, although they aren't very practical additions to a playground if not already on the site. The climbing surface and experience of rocks can be duplicated in concrete, which also can be shaped into sculptural forms. Two ways of using concrete in a play environment are the ferrocement technique and the "stack-sack" method (see Chapter 7 for building details).

ROPE, CHAIN, CARGO NET Soft materials such as rope, chain, and nylon cargo nets create climbers that move. A similar type of flexible environment is the suspended platform, which combines a hard-surfaced wooden platform with the moving support of chains (if hung from above) or springs (if supported from below). The dynamic factor of such environments makes climbing more challenging to children, and it provides muscle-programming experiences that differ from those offered by hard surfaces. Soft climbing environments also foster interaction among children, since one person's movement affects everyone else.

Because such soft materials as rope and

Chain ladder.

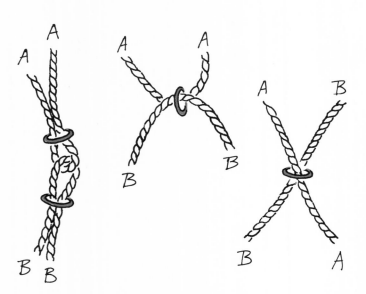

Three ways that ropes can be connected with metal rings.

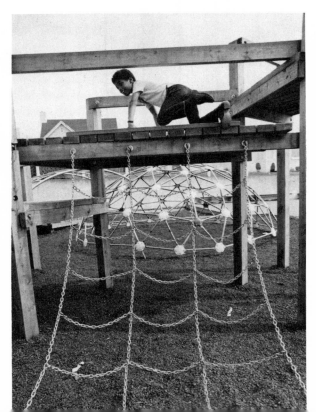

Bundling rope lessens confusion.

Square knots work well for rope net—two outer strands knotted around two inner strands.

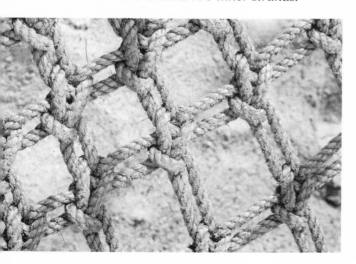

Net bridge between suspended plywood platforms.

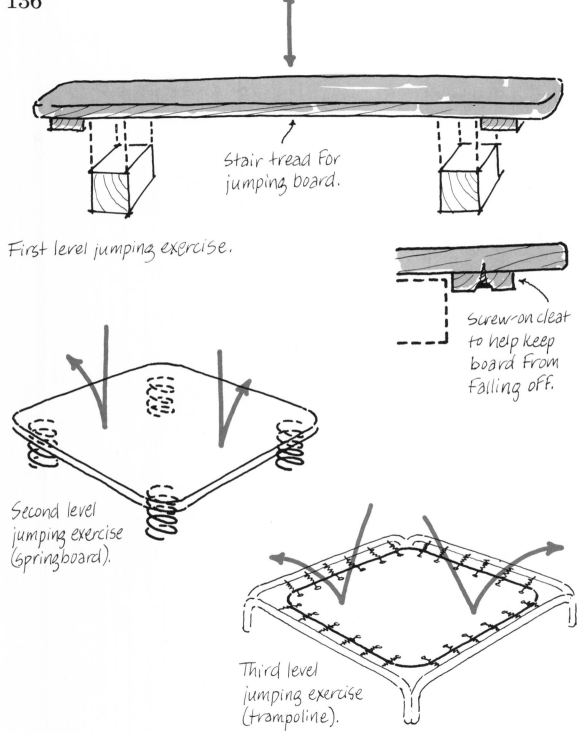

Stair tread for jumping board.

First level jumping exercise.

Screw-on cleat to help keep board from falling off.

Second level jumping exercise (springboard).

Third level jumping exercise (trampoline).

nylon stretch and shrink with use and exposure, some give-and-take must be built into these structures. A cargo net or knotted-rope climber can be stabilized and its slack taken up by tension ropes, which are attached to some permanent part of the play structure and can be tightened or loosened as necessary. Soft environments will last longer and retain their shape better with frequent maintenance and adjustment of the tension ropes.

Of the types of rope available, nylon, Manila, and polypropylene are most commonly used for outdoor play environments. Nylon rope, though expensive, is the first preference for playground use. It lasts well, is soft and pliable, and generally retains its shape even though it stretches. Manila is the second choice in rope; it is soft and workable, in addition to being much cheaper than nylon, but Manila doesn't last nearly so long as the synthetic ropes. The third choice of rope is polypropylene, which lasts well but is much less pliable than the others and can give kids plastic splinters when its fibers are somewhat worn.

If vandalism is a concern or absolute permanence is desired in a soft climbing environment, chain can be substituted for rope. The textural severity of chain can be alleviated by covering it with bicycle inner tubes or plastic hose.

Rope used to lash plywood panels to metal structure.

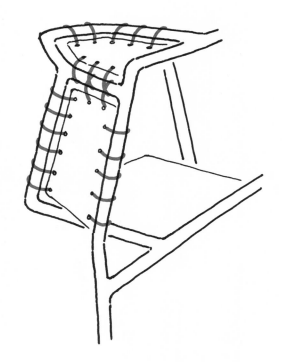

TIRES   Another source of flexible climbing structures is tires, which are initially free, but attaching them together properly and building adequate supports can be expensive. Tires make good nets and ladders, they can be shaped into a mound, and a huge tractor tire can be used for a sandbox. However they're used, tires must be well supported because they are heavy and tend to sag. Holes must also be cut in all tires to allow them to drain. Tires are best fastened together with chain, although they can also be bolted together.

Chain is the most reliable tire joint. Putting chain only around bottom side keeps top smooth for kids.

Bolting tires together is a time-consuming and difficult job.

Malleable washer

or

Fender washer

Double nuts

3/8-in. bolt

The double nuts lock against each other and prevent loosening.

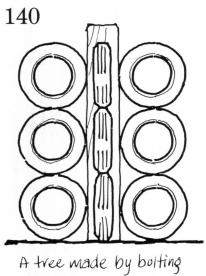

A tree made by bolting tires to a post.

The tree is hard to climb because the tires are soft and flop from side to side.

A better tire tree for the younger children is made by supporting the tires from both sides.

The bottom tires on a tall stack always squash.

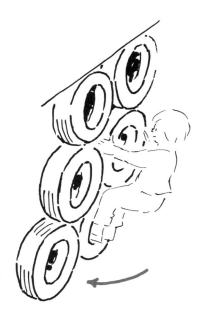

When tires are hung they require attachment at the base to prevent the nets swinging inward when children climb it.

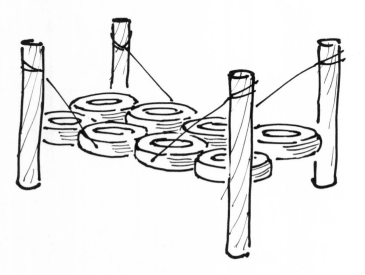

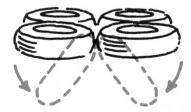

A tire bridge needs
support from the sides
or the weight of the
kids will cause it to
fold in the middle.

Tires bolted to telephone poles; use very stiff, thick tires.

Equipment for Quiet Play

It's really important for children to be able to close the door on the rest of the world sometimes, and quiet-play areas allow that to happen. Quiet play includes two kinds of privacy, for small groups and for individuals. Social or group privacy enhances interaction and fantasy play, which is stimulated by the visual and textural variety of the space. A child also will seek a kid-sized place, some little nook within a structure, where he can eat lunch or read a book or just be away from the commotion for a while. This individual privacy is especially needed in crowded urban communities, since the playground may offer the only opportunity for some children to be alone.

PRIVATE SPACES   A play structure can be designed to provide private spaces, such as the area between upper and lower platforms or an A-frame teahouse. A tunnel offers another kind of separation from the flow of traffic on the playground, and it's a sort of social equalizer, since everybody has to crawl through it. Tunnels can be made of metal barrels, concrete pipe, or wood, and kids especially like tunnels that are off the ground or under it (in a mound of dirt).

The topography of a play environment also can create private spaces. A quiet-play area could be set off by plantings or by a feature in the landscape, such as a hill.

145

Tunnel mound.

SAND AND WATER PLAY   Kids love to play with sand or dirt, and a sand and water area gives a new learning dimension to this play. A tub of sand to which water can be added allows children to investigate the properties of these natural materials. When dry, sand has no structural quality, but when a little water is added it can be shaped; too much water, though, and the sand won't hold any shape—it begins to resemble the water, in fact. Although they wouldn't know the word, kids are learning about synergy; the combination of dry, shapeless sand and wet, formless water into a structure that will take and hold shape shows them that two familiar things put together can make something quite new.

OUTDOOR MEETING PLACE   The playground should include an area that can be used for quiet play and for teaching. Children relate in special ways in an outdoor meeting space, and their play there is often instructive as well as contemplative. Two design features encourage sharing and interaction in such spaces—a seating arrangement that orients people toward one another, and screening from wind and noise so that people can speak at a conversational level and be heard.

STAGE   Another kind of social interaction is the presenting of self. Children often have a strong motivation for getting on a stage and acting out a story, and it's one of the social risks they need to take. Of course a stage can be used as part of the teaching process as well.

Outdoor meeting place.

Gazebo.

GAZEBO   A gazebo is by definition an open structure that looks out on something beautiful, and it can be an excellent place for quiet play. Such an area for contemplation and solitude shows the children that adults value these feelings enough to include a place for them in the play environment. In fact, these quiet places are distinctive parts of many cultures, such as the Japanese tea garden or the courtyard of a church, and they signify a respect for the individual and her thoughts that is important for everyone to learn.

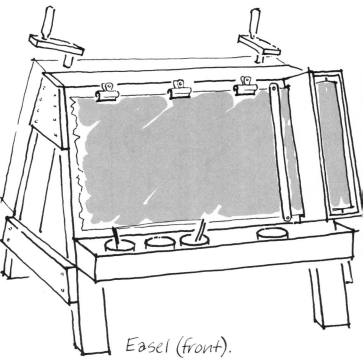

Easel (front).

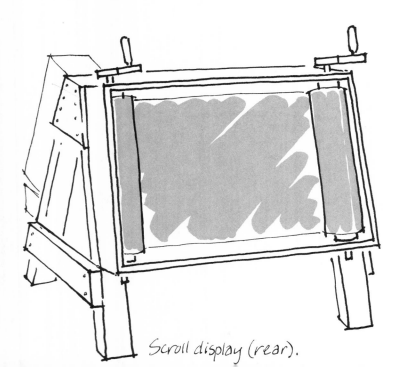

Scroll display (rear).

ARTS AND CRAFTS TABLE, EASEL
Quiet areas are well suited to learning, and with such equipment as an easel or a workbench, children can create things that will affect their own environment. The kids might make banners to hang on the play structure or wooden sculpture for one of the quiet areas in the space, for instance, or they might even design and build an addition to the main structure. Such activities are a continuation of the process by which the community created the playground, and they help fulfill the children's need to express themselves in the space around them.

Benches built with 6 x 6 remnants from play structures.

Miscellaneous Essentials

When a group of adults and kids plans a playground, the emphasis is generally on equipment and major structures. But some nonequipment features also contribute significantly to the value of a play space, and one thing, ground cover, is essential for its safe use.

PORTABLE STUFF   One sign of a kid-oriented play space is the portable stuff, the objects that kids can control and use to change the environment at will. Children can use these items to relate to the structure, such as leaning a plank up against it for an instant ramp, and they often involve such objects in their fantasy play. Among the possibilities for kid-controlled equipment are scrap metal (an old steering wheel, perhaps) and wood, a sawhorse, boxes (wood, plastic, cardboard), pieces of pipe and joints with which to put them together, loose tires, wooden or metal barrels, and costumes or pieces of fabric to use for that purpose.

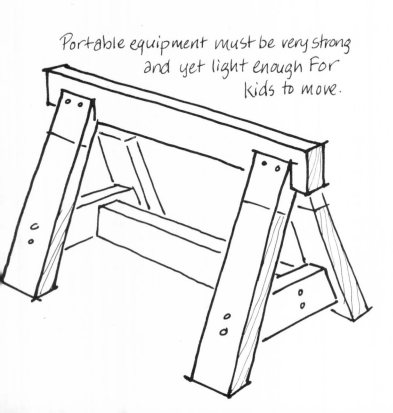

Portable equipment must be very strong and yet light enough for kids to move.

TRIKES   Another portable play object is the tricycle, and it is the mainstay of many nursery school playgrounds. In fact, trikes often tend to dominate play spaces, in the same way that cars often dominate much of the urban environment. Instead of being the means for getting from place to place, these conveyances can become the source of tension and controversy, whether it's a freeway traffic jam or a fight over whose turn it is on a trike. But if some alternatives are added to the environment, such as an active-play center for a nursery school, the tricycles will no longer be the center of attention but will take a more appropriate role in the children's play.

Trikes also can be quite expensive, particularly if a group buys the heavy-duty commercial models. There is a useful alternative to those costly metal tricycles, though—the plastic trike called a "Big Wheel." Besides being cheap and almost as durable as a metal trike, the plastic version forces its rider to use a whole different set of muscles from those used in other play activities; in contrast, on a standard tricycle a child exercises the same muscles used in running. A plastic trike is also more stable, since its low seat keeps the center of gravity close to the ground.

STORAGE   A child-oriented playground needs outdoor storage so that kids can have access to their portable objects and teachers don't have to drag the kids' things in and out of the building several times a day. Generally this storage space is used for wheel toys, portable stuff, and supplies for teacher-directed activities; each of these should be given a separate storage area. Trikes, bikes, and other wheel toys are best stored in a long, low shed, where children can easily get them in and out and where they don't have to be moved to permit access to anything else. The other two storage needs can be met with one large cabinet that has back-to-back compartments and doors on both sides. One side is for the kids' stuff, such as sand-play toys, costumes, wood scraps, and boxes; the other side holds things to which kids shouldn't have free access, such as scissors, paints that must be mixed, and modeling clay. Storage areas should be well planned in advance and built durably and securely, with framing comparable to that of a house.

GROUND COVER   Selecting ground cover for the playground can be the most exasperating design situation a group will encounter. The active-play area must have a shock-absorbing surface, at the very least under such equipment as swings and slides, but people have a hard time agreeing on what material to use. The best materials for ground cover are sand, tanbark (small pieces of tree bark), and rubber matting. Unfortunately they are all expensive and will probably take up about one-fourth of the group's budget. Grass and dirt, on the other hand, are not sufficient as shock-absorbing surfaces for active-play areas; grass will be destroyed very quickly and dirt is an out-of-control medium because it changes with the weather.

If the playground already has a hard surface (asphalt or concrete), any of the three ground covers can be used. Rubber must be placed on a hard surface, and although it is the most expensive of the materials, it can be used judiciously, thus bringing its cost to a comparable level with sand or tanbark. Rubber matting may be particularly good for a large public school, since either of the loose materials may be the source of objections from teachers and parents; sand usually finds its way into the classrooms, and some children may be allergic to the dust from tanbark. Sand goes well on a hard surface, but it requires a retaining wall, so the savings from its purchase may have to be used for the retainer. Sand does have the advantage, though, of being a play material in itself. Tanbark is less effective on a hard surface because it gets ground up with use and is easily pushed away from impact areas. It also requires a retaining wall. If the playground's surface is dirt, the sand or tanbark will have

to be more than 1 foot deep because the loose material will be pushed down into the soil as children play on it.

Maintenance of ground cover usually means replenishing the supply of sand or tanbark about every two years, since both of these materials tend to disappear from the play surface. One way to keep sand out of the classrooms is to build a slotted walkway (with ½-inch spaces between boards, say) from the playground to the school doors; this allows the sand to drop off the kids' shoes and clothes as they leave the play area. Sanitation is another factor to be considered when using loose ground cover, since it might be littered by dogs and cats. While this may be unpleasant, it hasn't proved to be a major problem in most community-built playgrounds and should be seen as an unavoidable aspect of modern living.

RETAINING WALLS   Ground-cover retainers can be an aesthetically pleasing part of the play environment. They may be made of wood or concrete, but whatever its design and material, the retaining wall should be at least 5 feet away from the play structure so that kids won't fall or jump onto it. This retainer should be 16 to 22 inches high to contain ground cover approximately 12 inches deep.

Wooden retaining walls are subject to rot and so must be built with redwood or with pressure-treated or creosote-treated wood, such as railroad ties. Since the chemicals used to treat wood are poisonous, however, a layer of untreated wood must be put on the top edge of the retaining wall to prevent direct contact with the poison. A wooden retainer might serve as outdoor seating, and its shape and texture can be varied as well. Log ends of different lengths might be placed vertically against each other to form both a retainer and a multilevel walkway, or concrete pipes might be set on end at several points within the wall to serve as planters.

A concrete retaining wall can be built with stack sacks—bags of dry concrete that are piled into the desired shape, strengthened with metal rod, then thoroughly wetted. After the concrete has hardened, the surface of the wall is plastered and can be painted or decorated with mosaics. The entire design process, much of the building, and all of the finishing of a stack-sack structure can be done by the kids.

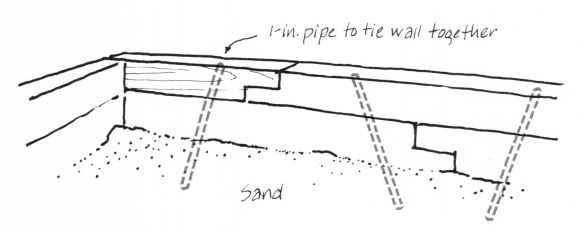

1-in. pipe to tie wall together

Sand

Railroad-tie sandbox with notched connections.

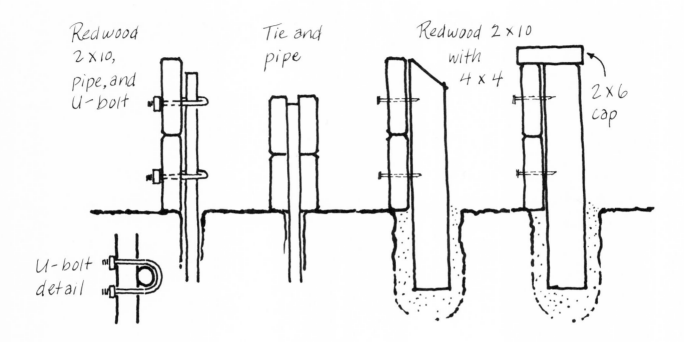

Redwood
2 × 10,
pipe, and
U-bolt

U-bolt
detail

Tie and
pipe

Redwood 2 × 10
with
4 × 4

2 × 6
cap

SAFETY RAILS   Parents and teachers usually think that safety rails are absolutely necessary to protect the kids on a play structure. But it's important to understand that children don't see a guardrail as a barrier, just as they don't recognize or use the railing along a stairway for support. Kids see the safety rail as just another place to play, and they will climb up on it and use it as a balance beam, which is potentially more dangerous than the hazards the railing is guarding against. Consequently, safety rails should be kept to a minimum. They should be installed on the outside edges of platforms from which there is more than a 4-foot drop and at points where a barrier is needed to slow up the traffic, such as at the top of a slide.

6 How Does It All Go Together?

Planning the Play Environment

Whenever changes are made in a space, the way people behave in that space inevitably will change too. At the simplest level, if a tree that shaded several benches is cut down, the way people use the benches will instantly change because the climate there has gone from cool and dark to hot and bright. If that tree was the only one in the area, the people who came there to get out of the sun will have to find another place to sit. But if whoever decided that the tree should be cut down had consulted those people first, they might have found a way together to keep their tree or at least to create a new source of shade.

In fact, the reason that many spaces, such as parks or malls, don't work well is precisely this lack of communication between the people making decisions about the space and the people using it. Spaces that do work well, on the other hand, are usually ones where the decision makers and the users are the same people. The difference between a Latin American barrio and an urban ghetto illustrates this point. A barrio gets better and better because the residents take charge of their environment. Since there is no one to do

it for them, the people build their own dwellings, slowly enlarging and improving them, adding plumbing and sewers, and in time making adequate living spaces out of what had been slums. In contrast is the high-rise tenement created by urban renewal, with little or no participation from the residents. These rather sterile, modern environments usually deteriorate because the people there have no control over the spaces where they must live.

The same is true for play environments. Someone from outside the community can come in and design a playground, but unless the people who will use it are involved in the planning, their attitudes about the space won't change with it. Thus, they'll try to re-

tain their old habits in the new environment, with the result that the playground will not be as safe or as socially beneficial as if those people's feelings had been expressed during the planning. In addition, if people get to participate in the planning for an environment, they come away with the feeling of gratification. Because the environment is of their own making, the community will take pride in it, and that's something no outside expert could ever give them.

So when planning for a playground, it's important that the community be involved as fully as possible. A group should develop a good system of communication so that everyone interested will have a chance to participate and to express his ideas and so that the community members can really consider what they want in a play environment. Establishing the communication mechanisms will be almost as big a job as building the playground, but the work will pay off in its broad representation of the community, with the potential for future use. If one aspect of a neighborhood's communication system is a telephone tree, for instance, the group will have an instant means of spreading the word and mobilizing residents on other issues that affect the community, such as changes in zoning or elimination of an area of open space. With such devices for keeping people in touch with one another, a community is much more likely to have a role in making decisions about the environment than if it had no such resources.

Specifically, creation of a play environment is a process of combining a community's

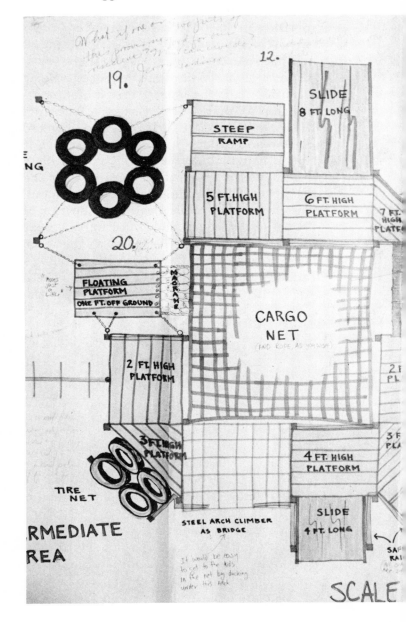

Detail of poster-sized plan with people's comments and suggestions.

self-image, concerns, and ideas with the available resources and design options. The decisions about how to put these elements together in a space seem somewhat arbitrary—the group simply decides one thing or another—but these decisions should be related to a whole evolutionary process. Some conditions of the space are more easily recognized, and the decisions concerning these can be made first. If the group plans to include an outdoor art area, for example, it should be near a water source, and if that's inside, the art area will have to be near the door from the building to the playground. This decision dovetails nicely with location of the basketball court, since the art area is next to the building and the ball-playing space must be well away from both the building's windows and the art space. Similarly, if there are some trees and bushes already in the space, this is the logical place for a quiet-play area.

A group's analysis of how to organize the play space should include three major criteria. First, the members will have to consider the functional needs of the playground in order of priority, that is, active play (including ball games), climbing, quiet areas, open space, storage, and so forth. Second, the group should determine the curriculum input for this space, by deciding what kind of social and learning experiences the children should be offered there, which also requires consideration of the staff time available for outdoor teaching and supervision. Third, the community must realistically examine its energy limitations. A group should of course try to plan for everything desirable in the

play environment, but the members probably won't be able to build it all at once. And because the community will grow and change during this initial phase of playground creation, it's wise not to spend too much time and energy on a detailed master plan at the beginning of the process.

Another important consideration in organizing space in the playground is how activities should be grouped. The adult tendency in arranging activities in a space is to separate them into neat, distinct areas, but the kids' perspective is quite different; they will see the activities as separate even if they are grouped closely together. An important objective is to integrate activities and thus promote social interaction. This can be done with paths and bridges, for instance, so that there is a built-in flow between experiences. Establishing such patterns of movement also serves to protect the fragile things in a space, such as landscaping, privacy, conversation, or teaching.

A group might broaden its perspective of the play environment by thinking of it as a total world, rather like the map of Pooh Corners in A. A. Milne's *Winnie-The-Pooh*. This drawing, made in the conceptual style of a child, is a complex world of spaces and places, although the basis for it probably was the author's back yard. Similarly, in a child's mind the playground can be a whole world, and from this vantage point, a playground of asphalt and steel is a desolate world, unless the people who care about the children's view make some changes and additions.

Finally, after a group has considered the

general goals and activities for the play environment, its members must answer some specific questions about the organizational aspects of that space. They need to determine the population of the environment, as well as the size and age of children there, so that the structures will be built to an appropriate scale for the kids. Other specific considerations include how supervision will be managed, if there is to be supervision, and how the physical features of the space, such

as a slight slope for drainage, will affect its use. (See the checklists in this chapter for detailed information.)

The considerations for planning a play environment have been listed here in a more-or-less chronological order, but a community group will probably have to go through them several times in the course of making decisions for the playground. A useful tool for this process is to make a simplified map of the space (such as the sample on pp. 160–161),

SAMPLE SITE MAP

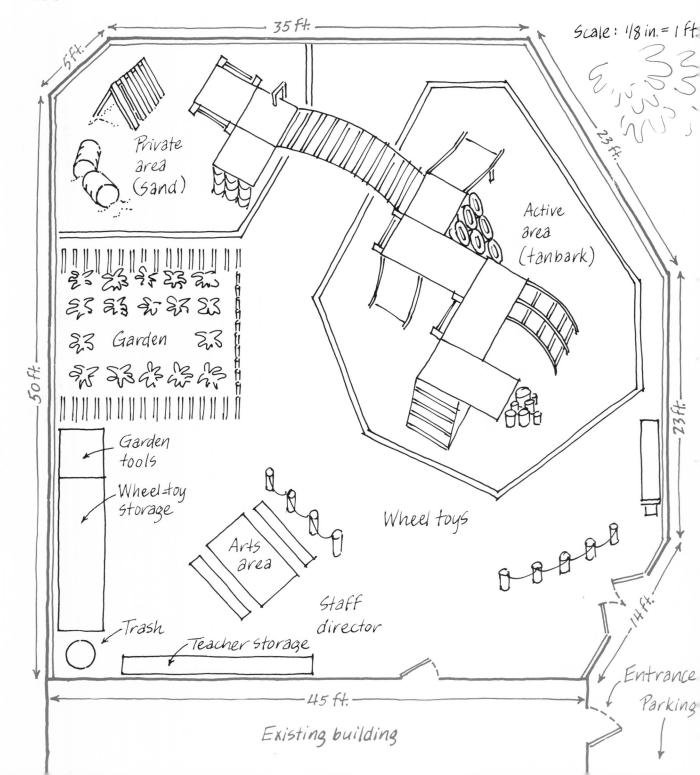

Scale: 1/8 in. = 1 ft.

35 ft.

5 ft.

23 ft.

Private area (sand)

Active area (tanbark)

Garden

Garden tools

Wheel-toy storage

Arts area

Wheel toys

Staff director

Trash

Teacher storage

50 ft.

23 ft.

14 ft.

Entrance

Parking

45 ft.

Existing building

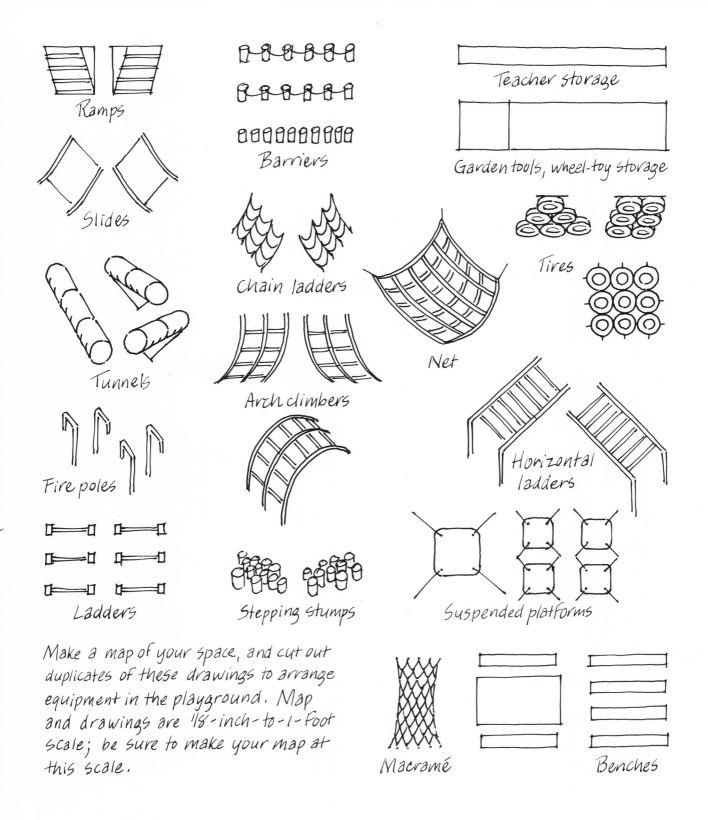

Ramps

Slides

Tunnels

Fire poles

Ladders

Barriers

Chain ladders

Arch climbers

Stepping stumps

Teacher storage

Garden tools, wheel-toy storage

Tires

Net

Horizontal ladders

Suspended platforms

Make a map of your space, and cut out duplicates of these drawings to arrange equipment in the playground. Map and drawings are 1/8-inch-to-1-foot scale; be sure to make your map at this scale.

Macramé

Benches

which can be duplicated and distributed with a list of possible activities and equipment for the playground. In this way everyone has a chance to do some preliminary designing, and the group can then take the most interesting ideas and find ways to fit them together.

Making It Happen

An efficient way to utilize the time and energies of people in the community group while gathering essential information about available resources and design options is to create committees for the three main areas of responsibility, namely, design, materials, and communications. If possible, the membership of these committees should overlap, or the groups should at least keep each other well informed.

DESIGN COMMITTEE   This group's job is basically educational, and the quality of information the members present will have a big influence on the outcome of the design process. Their first task is to research the possibilities for the playground, as well as the community's needs in such an environment, and report back to the whole group. While design options are fairly easy to find by visiting other playgrounds and doing library research, the committee also must thoroughly explore the ideas of community members, which may prove a bit more challenging.

Three tools will be most useful to this committee for involving the community throughout the design process; they are questionnaires, drawings, and models. A

questionnaire inventories opinions and creates an easy initial involvement for many people (see list of sample questions, p. 163). In addition, if the children help distribute questionnaires, by taking them home to their parents and perhaps passing them out to neighbors, there's a direct, personal link between the person being asked to complete the form and the source of its benefit, the kids. A questionnaire, though, is only as good

Sample Questionnaire: Inventory of Community Interests

(Duplicate and Distribute)

1. Complete the sentence: Our new playground should be _____
   _____

2. What could you learn by building a playground?
   (a) _____
   (b) _____
   (c) _____

3. What can kids do to help build a playground?
   (a) _____
   (b) _____
   (c) _____

4. In one sentence tell why it is important to live in a beautiful place. _____
   _____

5. Give an example of doing more with less.
   _____

6. What will happen when other communities hear about your playground?
   _____

7. How can new ideas be added to your playground after we have made the plans?
   _____

8. How can a playground be like:
   (a) a half-built house _____
   _____

   (b) a stream in the mountains _____
   _____

   (c) the beach _____
   _____

   (d) a mysterious forest _____
   _____

9. Which is most scary: (a) using a power saw; (b) asking a contractor for free wood; or (c) making a decision?
   _____

10. Name three feelings you think you will have when the playground is completed.
    (1) _____ (2) _____ (3) _____

11. If all the kids in the neighborhood stood side by side, how big a circle would they make?
    _____

as its questions, and those questions must be directed to everyone who will be affected by creation of the playground. Questions should be phrased to allow creative responses, rather than merely giving choices between one or two obvious things. A poor question, for example, is, "Should we have sand or rubber as ground cover?" A better question is, "Do you think children can learn from playing with sand?"

Drawings create another level of involvement, and they get people thinking in terms of space, rather than function of equipment. Another advantage of drawings is that they are an instructive and fun group activity, particularly when parents and kids work together. And the drawings can be good advertisements for the playground project, helping to inform the community, stimulate new ideas, and even raise money. Preliminary drawings have the disadvantage, however, of preconditioning people's ideas, perhaps tending to overinfluence a group's selection of a design system and thus narrowing the aesthetic choices to whatever can be represented in two dimensions on paper.

Models have the advantage of allowing people to think three-dimensionally, and they generally make it much easier to visualize how the kids will use the playground and to discover the little spaces and features that couldn't be seen in a drawing. Models should be built to scale, with materials that are representative of real ones. Kids often make beautiful structures with styrofoam and toothpicks, but such models are seldom buildable, nor do the children learn how real materials go together from this experience.

Anyone who builds a scale model with realistic materials, though, will get an initial indication of the construction process, including the need for accurate measuring and cutting of materials. An accurate scale model also can be helpful in estimating the amount of materials needed for the actual playground. Like drawings, however, models have the disadvantage of tending to solidify people's expectations for the playground, especially when the model is neatly done and

Model-making equipment and supplies: (clockwise) electric drill and bits; cardboard, knife, and string; wire and needle-nose pliers; hammer; white glue; tape measure; clamps and clothespins; model; miter box and backsaw; (rear) wood cut to 1-inch-to-1-foot scale.

handsomely displayed. And it's hard to incorporate those unexpected donations, such as tree trunks or scrap metal, into a model, although such things may strongly influence the final design.

A scale for playground models that works well is a ratio of 1 inch to 1 foot. Children can usually comprehend this relationship, whereas they might be confused by a scale of ½ inch to 1 foot. And while the 1-inch scale makes large, rather cumbersome models, it's easy to visualize a structure and to represent its equipment at this scale. These large models also photograph well for publicity purposes.

The final step in the creation of a design is generally construction drawings, commonly called blueprints. These technical drawings require an experienced draftsman, and while blueprints do provide more specific information as to how much material and what types of hardware will be needed, they are expensive and difficult for laymen to interpret. Also, building from blueprints greatly diminishes the spontaneity of design that might otherwise take place during construction.

MATERIALS COMMITTEE   This committee is responsible for the logistics of construction, beginning with a thorough canvass of resources and materials available in the community. If the group plans to buy materials through another organization, such as the school district or city government, the committee must find out and master the requisitioning procedures for ordering supplies. It also should set up an accounting system to keep track of the budget and should provide a mechanism for purchasing things on short notice, since a work crew may run out of lumber or hardware and have to buy more to finish the day's construction.

The materials committee is likewise responsible for having things ready for workdays. The members should see that the school building is open for use of rest rooms, drinking fountains, and so forth, and that electricity and water are available. This committee also arranges for delivery and storage of materials throughout the building process.

COMMUNICATIONS COMMITTEE
This committee has the most varied set of duties, and its work provides the continuity that is crucial to the playground's success. The members of this group are responsible for letting the community know about the project and for keeping information flowing during its various phases. They also are the money raisers, which often goes hand in hand with spreading the word of this playground project.

In addition, this committee handles communications within the community group, generating lists of volunteers, scheduling crews for the various workdays, and calling people to remind them of their work dates, as well as to tell them what clothes to wear and tools to bring (and to bring lunches if someone else is not providing food for the work crews). On site, the committee should keep track of everyone who comes; nametags could be issued to kids (perhaps only if they have brought an adult with them). This group also is responsible for having roving safety advisors present for all workdays.

The communications committee provides documentation for the project as well. From their lists of workers, they can easily determine how many man-hours it took to build the playground, for example. They should encourage people to take photos and movies of all phases of the project, and they might invite the local media to cover the workdays and perhaps the dedication ceremony for the playground.

COMMUNITY COORDINATOR   In addition to these committees, the group

Some Considerations for Playground Design

GOALS

Maximize choice and diversity
Grouping of equipment to provide choice of activities
Provide for active play, quiet play, free play, and staff-directed activity
Sensory stimulation—variety of textures, colors, shapes, sounds, smells
Variety of scale suitable for children—spaces that are large, small, open, closed, private, public
Range of challenge, difficulty, risk—give children a choice of activities to develop their own skills
Separate activities, i.e., kickball and planting areas—protect quiet play

Encourage individual development
Building environment that encourages social interaction, such as development of elaborate games based on layout of equipment
Sharing, such as cooperative play activities
Large-muscle development—stimulating sense of balance, coordination
Use of imagination, such as building sand castles, inventing dramas
Encouraging self-reliance, such as choosing degree of difficulty of activities
Developing social identity—sense that kids are unique individuals with special qualities

Relevance to learning
Seeing playground as place that expands the learning and teaching potential of the school
Ways that schoolyard changes can have meaning to children
Outdoor space can involve kids who aren't comfortable in the classroom

CRITERIA

Safety—during construction
Caution when using toxic materials, such as mixing concrete or using wood preservative
Using tools with proper safety instruction, such as power saws, drills
Material handling, such as lifting correctly
Removing all rough edges on playground structures
Window breakage—clean up all loose rocks after workdays

Safety—when in use
Structural strength
   materials of adequate size and strength
   proper joining of materials
   good design
Protective surfacing—sand, tanbark, synthetic materials
Avoiding designs that might result in serious accident or injury, such as falling from height onto an object below
Making enough changes so there is less competition for play equipment

Maintenance
Avoiding places that collect trash or are hard to clean
Use of durable materials
Adequate retaining of ground cover

Construction
Planning each phase so that it can be completed in one day with relatively unskilled labor
Recognizing the importance of logistics of materials and people, such as having enough people to hold heavy material while it is secured
Building so that additions are possible
Construction that lends itself to creative change by the children, such as addition of mosaics, paintings, flags

Theme (aesthetic choices)
Repetition of shapes or use of a motif
Choice of materials, such as recycled versus new
Placement of objects and equipment for balance and scale
Color and decoration
Visual impact on neighborhood
Craftsmanship
Formal, planned design or spontaneous, on-site design

Materials That Can Be Found For Free or Very Little

(*Sources*)

6,9	Regular and giant tires, not steel belted, and rubber trimmings for ground cover
3,10	Cable spools
3	Telephone poles
1,2,4	Sound dead trees—8 to 12 feet tall and 10 to 20 inches in diameter at the base, with as many branches as possible
	Logs from sound trees, 3 feet long or longer, with no branches
7	Scrap-steel pipe and other salvage
7	Steel drums, some with both ends removed, preferably with ends rolled or made smooth
5,6,8	Dozens of pieces of concrete pipe:
	24 to 36 inches in diameter, random lengths (for tunnels)
	36 to 48 inches in diameter, 18 to 40 inches long (for planters)
5,6	Tons of fill dirt
1,2,4	Tons of soil conditioner—may be chopped tree cuttings
2	Sewage sludge for fertilizer
1,2,4	Landscaping plants
5,6	100 square feet of cobblestone, brick, or broken concrete for paths
1,6	Large and attractive boulders
8,13	Sand, cement, concrete, mural materials (broken tiles and plates, shells, old jewels, etc.)
12	Cloth for flags, canvas
12	⅜-, ½-, and ¾-inch rope, nylon or Manila
12	Cargo nets, parachute, government-supply junk

SOURCES OF MATERIALS
(*Ask for discount*)

1 Park and recreation departments
2 Departments of public works
3 Utility companies
4 Tree-service companies
5 Building contractors
6 Trucking and heavy-construction contractors (especially with city contacts)
7 Scrap-metal salvage yards
8 Concrete-pipe manufacturers
9 Tire dealers, recapping services (especially trucks)
10 Industrial-hardware dealers (especially wire rope)
11 Nurseries
12 Government surplus
13 Sand, gravel, and concrete suppliers

TOOLS

Each worker should bring: tape measure, hammer, gloves, and pencil (do not bring light-duty, household-type tools).

Experienced workers should bring: those heavy-duty tools that would be used in normal house-construction carpentry. MARK YOUR TOOLS.

Other hand tools: assorted wrenches, including socket and vise grip; chain cutters; dirt tools (shovels, picks, bar, posthole digger)

Trucks: dump, stake, and/or pickup.

Heavy equipment: bulldozer, skiploader, backhoe.

Miscellaneous equipment: power generator, jackhammer, two-man posthole digger, pipe bender, chain saw, welding gear, wheelbarrows, heavy-duty extension cords (#12, 3-wire).

should select a coordinator, who will be the effective leader for all phases of the project. This person should expect to invest a great deal of time in the playground project, since he or she will sit on all three committees and no doubt will be the person who is called long after the playground is completed if anything needs maintenance or if someone from another neighborhood wants to start a similar process.

"Typical" Examples

The first two examples here are based on the combined experiences of many groups, and the following situations are representative of what any community might expect when creating an environment for play.

NURSERY SCHOOL At the fall meeting of parents and staff of this co-op nursery school, the head teacher told the group that the children's outdoor play area was inadequate and that the staff would like the parents' help in creating a better playground. At that time, the play equipment consisted of trikes, which had to be taken in every night, a swing set, and a sandbox. The school served thirty-five families, of whom ten were single parents, and had two daily sessions; twenty-two children, age 3½ to 4½, came for the morning only, and eighteen kids, age 4½ to 5½, stayed all day and had lunch at the school. The fees were $85 per month for children who stayed the full day and $40 per month for a half day. In addition, each parent was required to work at the school for four

hours a week assisting the staff of three teachers.

The parents voted to form a playground-improvement committee, for which five parents and one teacher volunteered. During the next month, the members of this group visited several playgrounds in the area, did some reading about play, and made an inventory of basic needs for the playground. Their report recommended areas for active play, climbing, and quiet play, an area for storage of the trikes and one for art activities, plus a drinking fountain. They also listed the problems complicating improvement of the play area, which included the fact that the schoolyard is used by neighborhood children, so the structures and storage area should be made secure; the site had poor drainage; and it would benefit from creation of a shelter against bad weather.

The group had $1,000 on hand at the beginning of the second month of planning. The parents held a fund-raising event that brought in another $750, then went to the city parks department to ask for matching funds. The parks director referred them to the council, so the group asked to be put on the agenda for a council meeting in four weeks. The members were advised to prepare complete plans to present at this meeting, so the committee canvassed all the families for their opinions, listed all the activities desired, then built a model of the active-play structure and made drawings of the other areas to be added to the playground. The committee also prepared a budget for the entire project, which totaled $4,500.

During the third month, the group pre-sented the model and drawings to the city council, which agreed to match the $1,750 the school had for the project. But the council also sent the group to the city maintenance department for approval of the structure, whose requirements added another $1,000 to the budget, so the group was $2,000 short, even with the city money. The parents voted to eliminate the drinking fountain, which lowered their budget by $500 in plumbing costs (they couldn't do this work themselves because of building-code restrictions), then started raising money and hustling materials. The committee got $150 from the Chamber of Commerce, a hardware discount worth $100, and a donation of 1,000 board feet of 2 × 6 lumber, which saved another $400.

In the fourth month, December, the school raised $800 at a Christmas sale, leaving the group only $50 short of the budget. During this month the committee also was given some broken concrete and a number of pine logs, which were 15 feet long and averaged 12 inches in diameter. The group decided to change the structure's design to incorporate the logs and to make a walkway with the broken concrete. The project was then ready to go, but since the winter weather had set in, the parents and staff reluctantly scheduled their two construction weekends for early April.

In late March, the committee ordered materials, and during the week before the first workday, two truckloads of dirt were delivered to the site. Several fathers and some neighborhood kids spent two evenings that week shaping some of the dirt into mounds. On the first workday, twelve people showed

(For Use by the Design Committee)

SITE

How large is the play space?

Are the entrances to your site beautiful?

Where does the water go after it rains?

Is there a problem with mud or sand being tracked into the building?

From what direction does the wind come?

What existing play equipment can be incorporated into a new play structure?

Where are the sunny and shady areas?

Will there be problems with noise?

How many children will be using the space during school and after school?

What is the range of the children's ages?

How is the area supervised?

Are there any other special problems with the site?

RESOURCES

What is your potential for scrounging materials: good, fair, or poor?

What is your potential for fund raising?

How many weekends do you think people can come out to work?

Who has carpentry skills?

Who has access to tools?

Who is your materials coordinator?

Who is your work crew coordinator?

Have you developed a schedule for planning sessions, preliminary designs, models, blueprints, and workdays?

Assemble as many donated and scrounged items as you can and find a secure place to store them. Then you can determine what you will have to buy.

GENERAL COMMENTS

Have some members of your group visit other community-built playgrounds. Take children along and watch them on the equipment. Ask them to tell you what they liked and what they would enjoy as part of their own play equipment. What do you notice about how the children interact on different pieces of equipment and in different kinds of spaces?

QUESTIONS TO ASK AFTER MAKING MODEL OR DRAWINGS

What would a five-year-old kid like about your design? A twelve-year-old?

What paths are there through your design? Over? Under? Around?

Does every path have several entrances and exits?

What areas of your design have two or more functions (uses)?

What large material would do the same job as your model-making materials?

What is the best way to make the joints in the structure you've designed?

What other material could be added to the structure by the kids who will use it?

What is the weakest point in your structure?

What parts of the play space can kids help build?

What will be the first thing to change in the play space?

What is there for old people to do in your playground?

Is there danger from cars near the playground?

What will be the effect of the playground on the neighboring houses?

up. They dug postholes, applied creosote to the logs, and set them in cement in the holes. Then the crew cleared out all the branches, weeds, and junk around the yard and tore down the old storage shed. Finally the workers graded some of the leftover dirt into a smooth surface on one side of the yard.

Fifteen people came on the second workday. They got the platforms and safety rails built onto the structure, built the horizontal ladder but didn't have time to install it, and did some landscaping around the playground's perimeter.

During the next week, two fathers came

after work for three days to lay the concrete walkway. On the first day of the second weekend, twenty-five people arrived. They put metal barrels in the dirt mounds; cut the tops off the posts and used them to hold the barrels in place; installed the horizontal ladder; made a wide slide and attached it to the structure; sanded and planed the structure's surfaces; and built the frame for the storage shed. Only six people showed up the next day. They put sealer on the wooden structure; put doors on the storage shed; did some planting in the nature area; and cleaned up the whole yard.

The playground was finished, and on Monday the kids were all over it. Even the quiet, shy ones were exploring and yelling back and forth with the others. The teachers and parents were proud and pleased, and they immediately began talking about their next project, a sheltered area and the drinking fountain. A few mornings later, someone discovered that a board had been broken; a father was called and he came after work and replaced it. That evening he called two other parents and the three of them agreed to serve as a maintenance committee; one person would check the playground every month and make any necessary repairs or adjustments.

ELEMENTARY SCHOOL This was a large public school including kindergarten through sixth grade. It had some state funds for an experiment in open classrooms and a member of the Teacher Corps was active there; in fact, he suggested improving the playground and was immediately supported by a group of parents who had tried to get an art program going in the school. At that time the playground was three-fourths asphalt and one-fourth poorly maintained turf; the only activities were ball games and a set of turning bars. There was a row of trees in front of the school, but none behind it where the play area was located. The school's problems included a lack of parent participation, especially among minority groups, and not enough ways for parents to become involved; some vandalism of the school and yard; a need for curriculum enrichment; lots of complaints about what happened to kids on the asphalt playground, such as scrapes, torn clothing, and too many fights; and a desire for two playgrounds so that the little children could have an area away from the big kids, although everybody realized that the second playground would have to come later.

The Parents Club approved the project and voted its $1,000 for the budget, and several parents and teachers volunteered to serve on a committee to investigate alternatives for a new play environment. This group made a list of the school's needs and wants for the playground, then suggested that the Parents Club form three separate committees to get the project under way. One parent who was a building contractor volunteered to head the materials committee, and a design professor from the local college agreed to help with the design. A teacher and a parent acted as cochairmen of the communications committee, and the Teacher Corps man was made coordinator for the project.

In the first phase of the project, the design committee took the wants and needs list and made a large drawing that incorporated all the ideas so far, then posted this in the cafeteria with a sign asking everybody to add comments and suggestions to the sheet. The materials committee got a donation of a large concrete pipe, five large tree trunks with some branches left on each, and a cargo net. The communications committee got two articles in local papers about the project.

During the second planning phase, the design committee took the comments and ideas from the large poster and made them into sketches, then organized a kids' workshop to build models of the proposed wooden play structure. A teacher also worked with other children to make clay models of concrete sculpture for the playground. The materials committee found storage space for materials in the school district's maintenance yard, and each student was given a list of materials needed for the playground to take home from school. The communications group took the wooden and clay models to a local television station, where two parents and two children described the project on a news program and appealed for donations of money and materials.

During the third phase, the design committee made a materials list and budget, which called for $1,500 worth of lumber

(including a discount), $500 in hardware, $500 for concrete, and $1,000 for commercial play equipment. In addition to getting a discount on lumber, the materials committee obtained all the sand the group would need for free (100 cubic yards) and fifteen long telephone poles, donated by a local power company, for the sand-retaining wall. The communications committee, meanwhile, got a $1,000 donation from the Kiwanis Club. So the group needed $1,500 to complete the budget for the playground. The principal allocated $500 from the school's maintenance fund, and the Parents Club decided to use the $200 it would have spent on Christmas lights and decorations for the playground project; individual donors gave $500 more, and the student council provided the remaining $300 for the budget.

In the fourth phase, the professor who headed the design committee donated his time in making blueprints of the playground for approval by the school board. The board did approve the plans but said that no platform could be higher than 8 feet (some had been higher), so the blueprints were amended to meet that specification. The materials people requisitioned materials for the building days and arranged for the school to be open on those weekends. The communications committee developed a telephone tree, prepared a list of volunteers for work crews, and made flyers announcing the workdays, which kids distributed to local stores. The two local papers again publicized the project.

Phase five was the last stage of preparation. The design committee measured and painted marks on the asphalt where posts were to be set. The materials group picked up supplies that couldn't be delivered, and the communications people called all the people in the project to remind them to be on site for the first workday.

Finally the workday arrived, and the design committee members organized the crew and posted a list of jobs. The materials committee rented some tools and borrowed others, while the communications group arranged for a free lunch and coffee and donuts for a morning break. The building took three weekends, with crews ranging from twenty to fifty people, including kids, who did many of the jobs on site. The father who was a builder and the Teacher Corps teacher acted as construction foremen; they told people how to carry materials and use tools properly and at times yelled for them to work harder.

This on-site leadership was necessary to keep the building going at a good pace, and these experienced persons also helped solve the problems that inevitably arose. Throughout the planning and construction of this playground, the builder, the design professor, and the Teacher Corps man shared the successive roles of a consultant whom the group might have hired if the members had not included such experienced persons. These roles included a directive function; a teaching role; the consulting role of being able to spot a problem and help the group focus on it; anticipating problems and keeping the pace going; and finally, remaining involved as simply a member of the group rather than the leader or expert.

Some Considerations for Writing a Contract

(Between the Community, a Consultant, and the Owner of the Site)

Responsibilities generally assumed by the community:
Insure good attendance at planning meetings and on workdays.
Provide sign-up sheet and nametags for kids that say which adult is their sponsor during the workdays.
Evaluate the progress of the project and make the necessary adjustments to the schedule and budget so that all of the work undertaken is completed.
Provide documentation and media coverage.
Have an annual paint-up/fix-up session to keep the playground fresh and in sound condition.
Arrange for emergency cash for last-minute purchases during workdays.
Bring tools, rent equipment, pick up "will call" orders.
Provide lunch.
Provide some portion of the money required to construct the playground.

Responsibilities a consultant might assume:
Provide information on play, playgrounds, and design alternatives.
Explain principles of design, characteristics of materials, and logistics of construction.
Provide sketches and specifications.
Construct model.
Work with kids on some or all of the above procedures.
Create architectural renderings (blueprints).
Provide material lists, write requisitions, select material suppliers.
Work on site with the community as job captain to provide coordination, teach use of tools, help make on-site design changes, and keep the project on schedule.

Responsibilities the owner may assume:
Make available information on limitations, i.e., height limitation, preferred ground cover, maintenance and safety considerations.
Approve plans, on-site changes, and budget.
Have a representative at meetings and workdays.
Inspect project during construction and after completion.
Provide all or part of cost of materials and consultant fees.
Maintain insurance necessary to protect persons and property during and after installation of equipment. (This is not as difficult as you might believe.)
Maintain and repair equipment after installation or coordination with the community for such maintenance.

COMMUNITY PARK   The three-committee system works well for a neighborhood park, although there is usually a less coherent body of people to work with than the parents and staff at a school. The design process may be somewhat slower than for either of the other two playgrounds because of the neighborhood's diverse elements, but it's particularly important that everyone in the area have a chance to participate in this phase of the project. The primary differences between the community park project and others are that the communication process is more difficult and the approval procedures are more complex, since a neighborhood generally has less leverage with the local government than the parents have in a school. Consequently, the community group must have good drawings, models, and blueprints, and the structures probably will have to conform precisely to the plans, rather than allowing the workers the freedom to add new materials at the last minute, as a school group might do.

Since this is a public park, the group will probably want to do more than build a play structure in the space, but the first priority for preserving any natural environment there is to provide a place for active play. If such an active center is not built, and the kids still congregate in the park for lack of anywhere else to go, the landscaping and grass or whatever is there will take a beating. After the active-play need has been met, some areas for privacy should be provided, since that is another essential for children. Then the community group can add picnic tables, lighting, more planting, or whatever the residents want.

A community garden, now the site of redevelopment housing.

7 "Where's My Hammer?"

When the planning is finished and the materials have been purchased, the long-anticipated building process can begin. That first workday is usually a time of exhilaration mixed with apprehension for most people; they're eager to transform the playground into the place they envision, but they also may be a bit frightened, and perhaps awed, at the task they've undertaken. Once the work begins, though, everybody's too busy to be scared.

Following a few basic guidelines will help make the workdays productive, safe, and satisfying for everyone in the group. First, the logistics of construction should be well thought out for a reasonably smooth building operation. Second, procedures should be developed for the proper use of tools and handling of materials, and no one should be permitted to deviate from them. Finally, since this is an unfamiliar situation for most people in a work crew, each person should be reminded to be careful in his actions, considerate of others, and realistic about his strength and endurance; instead of trying to do too much alone, a crew member should always ask for help. Additional workdays can be scheduled if the building is going more slowly than desired, and that's vastly pref-

erable to having someone get hurt because she's hurrying to finish a job or lifting materials when she's really too tired.

Division of Labor

Another important factor in the construction process is use of labor. One or two people always seem to complain that there aren't enough tools, which may mean that these people want to work with tools that others are using or that the jobs to be done haven't been well organized. In fact, one power-saw operation could involve eight people—two to carry lumber from its storage area, one to measure and mark the required lengths, two more to move the marked wood onto sawhorses for cutting, one person to operate the saw and one to teach and supervise its operation, and one person to carry the cut pieces to the part of the structure where they will be used.

An efficient way to organize the work crew is by division into small teams for specific tasks, such as the power-saw operation. The crew foreman, who's in charge of all work, might assign an experienced person to each team (if there are enough such people), and team members could trade individual jobs or trade places with someone on another team at various times during the day. The foreman and some members of the materials and design committees could prepare a list of jobs to be done each workday and post the list, as well as the plans for the playground, in a convenient, sheltered place. If the group is working from blueprints, of course, the foreman or others who are familiar with such

drawings may need to interpret them as the work progresses.

A list of jobs kids can do also should be posted, and perhaps some older children could help organize the kids into teams or keep them busy when they want to be. (Many children will work diligently all day; others will work for a while, play for a while, then come back for more work.) Kid jobs include carrying materials, measuring (with help, perhaps), filling holes in the structure with putty, nailing, counting hardware and other materials, picking up scraps and consolidating them into one pile, and spreading dirt or ground cover.

The foreman and team leaders also should try to keep the work going at an orderly pace. If people are hurrying or some team members don't seem to be paying attention to their work, the leader can have everyone stop and take a break, and maybe switch jobs with another person. Another wise precaution on workdays is to ask that people not have alcoholic beverages on site, or at least to limit their use to lunch time and cleanup.

Safety During Construction

PREPARATIONS Careful preparation for a workday can help insure the crew's safety and avoid confusion if there is an injury. One way the group could prepare to handle an emergency is by having an instruction session on first aid before the building begins. Members of the local fire department or Red Cross usually will come to a community meeting to give such a presentation. The group also should get a basic medical kit and establish a procedure for accident or emergency, such as posting the location and phone number of the nearest hospital.

Crew members should be told how to dress for safe work with power tools. People with long hair should tie it back or cover it with a scarf or close-fitting cap. Workers should not wear loose clothing, dangling jewelry, or anything else that might get caught in a power tool as they're using it. All crew members should have work gloves for rough work.

CREW FOREMAN The crew foreman should be experienced in tool use and safety. The group may wish to consider hiring (or convincing to volunteer) an on-site foreman who is not a group member, since an outside person generally can direct people and correct their mistakes with less personal conflict. This leader can teach crew members the proper use of tools and handling of materials, perhaps starting each workday with an instruction session. The foreman should not get too involved in working himself, but rather should keep the teams working steadily, give individual help with tools and materials, and help solve problems as they arise.

SAFETY ADVISORS In addition to the foreman, it's wise for a group to have several roving safety advisors, who have building experience and can help crew members handle tools and materials properly. A good ratio is one advisor for every ten workers. Some of the older, more responsible children might also help other kids work safely and efficiently.

MATERIAL HANDLING   Besides being taught to use tools safely, the crew should be instructed in the proper ways to handle materials. The correct way to lift something is to keep one's back straight, bend at the knees, and lift with the legs. A person should never bend over from the waist to lift a heavy object, as this puts all the strain on her back. People should be encouraged to ask for help if something is too heavy, and no one with a back problem should be allowed to lift heavy objects. Also, since most crew members are weekend builders at most, everyone should be urged to quit working when tired and to rest frequently.

Coordination of effort is also essential for a team that is handling large, heavy objects. If several people are carrying a big beam, for instance, the team leader can make the operation go smoothly by directing their movements, telling them to move forward or turn a few steps to the right, and talking constantly to keep a steady pace and to encourage them. If a large piece of material must be moved a fairly long way, the team should move it in increments, lifting and setting it down at the leader's direction.

TOOL USE   A work crew should always include an experienced foreman and, if possible, several other people who also are familiar with tools. If a group does not include such people, at least some members should learn

how to use the necessary tools before the playground construction is begun. There are many good reference books available on tool use and safety; among them are *How to Work with Tools and Wood,* by Robert Campbell (Pocket Books, $1.25); *Basic Carpentry Illustrated,* by the Editors of Sunset Books and Sunset Magazine (Lane Books, $1.95); and *Carpentry and Building,* by Harry F. Ulrey (Audel Guides, $5.95).

Two fundamental rules apply to the use of any kind of tool. First, a person should be in the proper position before beginning work with the tool; he should be balanced, with stable footing, and should hold the tool by

SAFETY IS NO ACCIDENT

Wear suitable work clothes and protective shoes.

Tie back hair or loose clothing.

Use three-wire (grounded) heavy-duty electrical cord.

Don't use power tools on wet ground.

Support wood correctly so that it doesn't pinch your saw.

Use protective goggles and gloves when necessary.

Lift correctly - with your knees, not your back.

Keep tools sharp.

Work at an even pace. Don't try to rush your job.

Don't try to work when you're tired. Most accidents happen late in the day.

Relax!

the proper handles. Second, no one, even an experienced builder, should be permitted to use a tool the wrong way. If someone is doing it wrong and claims it's okay because he knows what he's doing, he should be reminded that the kids and inexperienced persons need to see it done the right way.

An exhaustive list of tools and instructions for their use would be too long and too repetitious of other good information sources, such as the books already mentioned, to be practical here. The discussion that follows concentrates on specific problems that may be encountered with certain tools during playground construction.

PERSONAL SAFETY EQUIPMENT: Anyone using power tools, especially saws, or breaking asphalt or dirt with a pick should wear goggles or a face mask. A person using a chain saw should also wear ear protectors.

HAMMER: When using a hammer, relax and let gravity bring the hammer down and drive the nail; use the whole arm, instead of getting too close and concentrating on hitting the nail head. When pulling out a nail, put one hand over the spot where the nail will come out so it doesn't go flying. Don't let kids hit hammerheads together—they will shatter and send pieces of metal flying.

A small block improves leverage for nail removal.

CHISEL: The chisel is very sharp and should be stored out of kids' reach. It should be used with a mallet, not a hammer, and replaced to storage immediately after use.

Keep tools sharp.

Teamwork increases safety.

POWER SAW: The circular saw should be left in place after the power is turned off until the blade stops spinning; a common problem is the saw blade cutting its cord when someone moves the saw before the blade is still. Make only straight cuts with this saw; it doesn't turn corners.

DISC SANDER: This power tool also may cut its cord (or something else), so it should be held on the surface being sanded until the disc stops completely. Because it is a heavy and unwieldy tool, the person using the disc sander should get into a balanced position before turning it on.

Watch that cord!

ELECTRICAL CORDS AND PLUGS: Extension cords should be the minimum length necessary to reach the work area because long cords cause a loss of power, which will result in blown fuses and damage to tools. Only #12 grounded wire should be used. If it's at all wet (morning dew on the ground, for example), electrical tape should be put around plugs and extension-cord joints to prevent water from getting into a plug. If any tool gives off even the slightest shock or seems to be working improperly, it should be taken out of service immediately. All cords and plugs should be inspected each workday and any bad or questionable ones taken out of service.

WOOD PRESERVATIVE: Creosote and other wood preservatives are poisonous and toxic to skin and eyes, so anyone using them should wear rubber gloves and be very careful. Kids should not be allowed to handle these chemicals, and the containers and brushes should be stored securely when not in use.

ON-SITE DESIGN Nearly every project requires some modifications in the playground plans during construction, and certain precautions will help insure the safety of these spontaneous designs. The structure should always be inspected to see that there is nothing sticking out that kids might run into and to be sure that all passageways are wide enough for two children to pass.

Building with Wood

After digging postholes and cleaning the site, dispose of rocks and cover holes to prevent mishaps.

Three steps in attaching beam to post: (1) using power saw to make series of cuts for notch (left); chiseling wood from series of cuts, thus creating notch (center); countersinking (foreground), the first drilling operation for bolting beam to post in notch.

Leveling and marking for safety-rail notch.

Laying 2 x 6 decking on 4 x 8 beams. Decking should be laid with heartwood facing down. (To find the heartwood, look at the end of the board for the rings with smallest diameters—these indicate the center of the tree and should be placed downward.)

Boards without proper center support will bend, causing nails to lift.

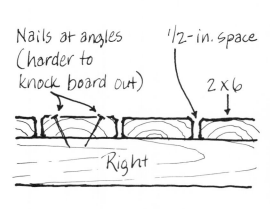

Nails at angles (harder to knock board out)

1/2-in. space

2 x 6

Right

Look at end grain of boards. Smaller rings go face down.

Wrong

Use planes to round edges of lumber.

After filling bolt holes with exterior water-base drying putty, paint all wood surfaces with this wood-preserving finish: 1 gallon penetrating oil (such as Penetrol), 1 gallon penetrating water seal, 1 gallon paint thinner, 2 gallons boiled linseed oil. Mix well. CAUTION: *mildly toxic*

Tools

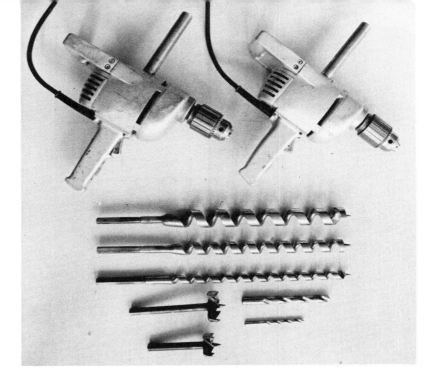

Drills: 1/2-inch reversible electric drills; auger bits; countersinking bores (bottom left); and metal-boring bits (bottom right).

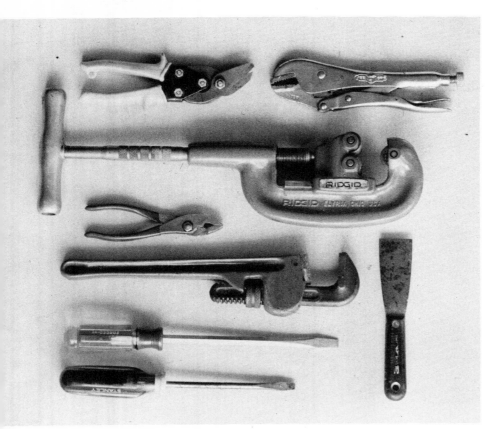

Various hand tools: tinsnips (top left); vise grip (top right); pipe cutter; pliers; pipe wrench; screwdrivers; putty knife.

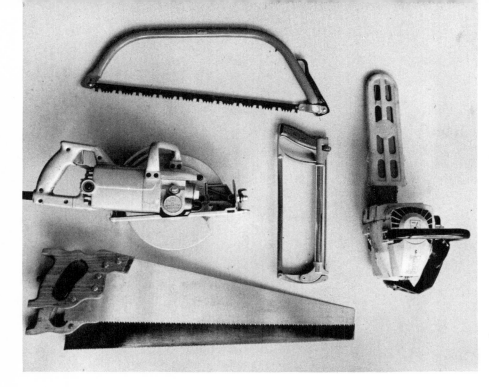

Saws: (clockwise, from top) bow saw; chain saw; rip and crosscut hand saws; power saw; hacksaw (center).

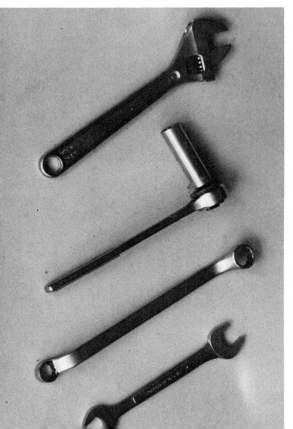

Wrenches: (from top) crescent; socket; box; open-end. (The latter three come in sets.)

Nailing tools: (from left) nail puller; small sledgehammer; claw hammer; crowbar; nippers (for pulling nails).

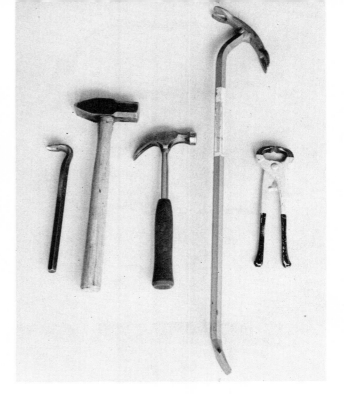

Surfacing tools: (left row, from top) jack plane; surform; block plane; drawshave; (center row, from top) whetstone; knife; file; gouge; chisel; (right) wooden mallet for use with chisel.

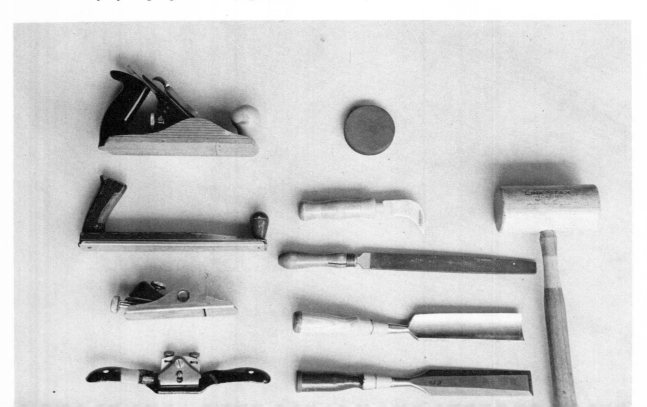

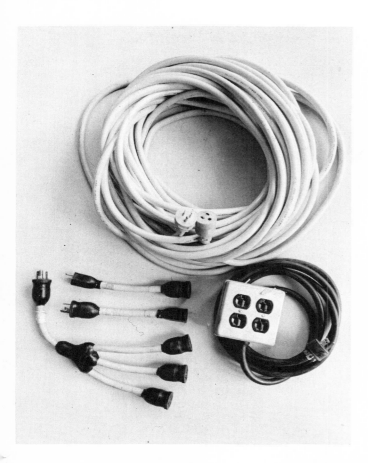

Electrical cords: (top) three-wire #12 extension cord; (center left) straight-to-twistlock-plug ("pigtail") adapters; (bottom left) branch; (right) extension with four-outlet box.

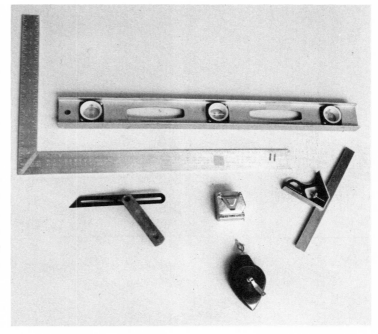

Measuring tools: (from top) level; framing square; (bottom left) sliding T-bevel; (center) tape measure; (bottom center) chalk line and plumb bob; (right) combination square.

Duplicate these pages and post on site.

Wrong

Right—stand back and swing.

No two-handed pounding

Wrong

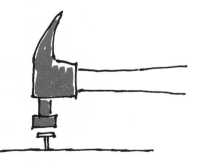

Right—hit the nail squarely.

Wrong - causes
wood to pinch
saw.

Right

Diggers: shovel; iron bar; pick;
posthole digger; sledge; hoe.

Don't forget—wheelbarrow, sawhorses, ladder.

Hardware

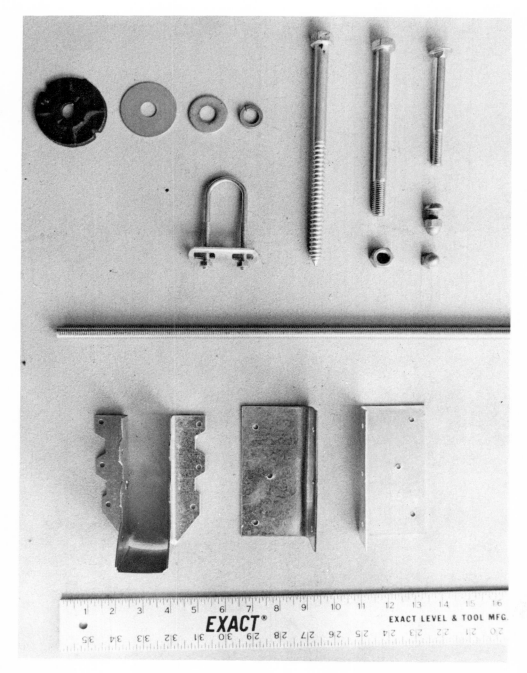

Connectors: (top row, from left) malleable washer; fender washer; lag screw; hex-head bolt with nut; carriage bolt, with acorn nut and screw below; (top center) U-bolt; (center) threaded rod; (bottom row, from left) universal hanger; sheet-metal right angles (two views). (Bottom—scale in inches.)

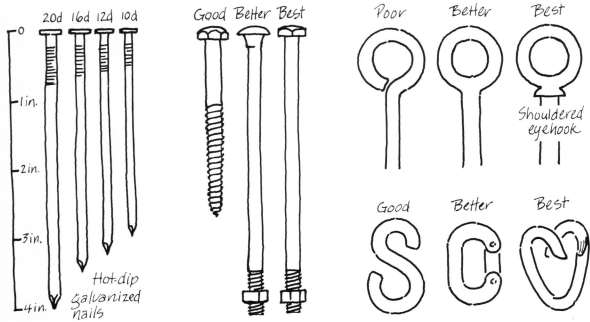

20d 16d 12d 10d

0

1 in.

2 in.

3 in.

4 in.

Hot-dip galvanized nails

Good Better Best

Poor Better Best

Shouldered eyehook

Good Better Best

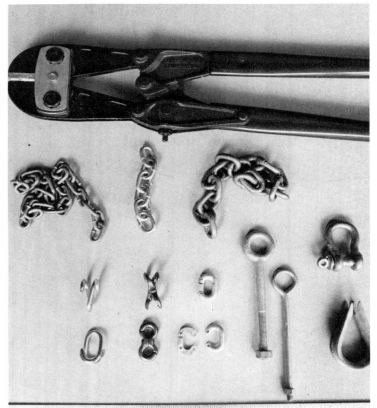

5 6 7 8 9 10 11 12 13 14 15 16 17 18 19 20 21 22 23 24 25

EXACT   EXACT LEVEL & TOOL CO., Inc.   HIGH BRIDGE, N. J., U.S.A.

Chain and equipment: (top) chain cutter; (top row) chain samples, various sizes; (bottom rows) two views of three chain fasteners; eye bolts; (right center) shackle; (right bottom) thimble. (Bottom—rule for scale in inches.)

Sample Material-Ordering List

LUMBER

Lumber size	Actual size	Number of pieces	X length	= lineal feet	X factor*	= board feet	Lumber grade	Price	Cost
2x4	1½x3½				0.33				
2x6	1½x5½				0.1				
2x8	1½x7½				1.33				
4x4	3½x3½				1.33				
4x6	3½x5½				2				
6x6	5½x5½				3				

* factor is the number of board feet (1 square foot of lumber, 1 inch thick).

Subtotal _____

Tax _____

Delivery _____

Total _____

All lumber should be Douglas fir or equivalent, surfaced on all four sides (S4S).
_____ sheets _____ inch-thick plywood (exterior grade, good on one side)

NAILS (come in 50-pound boxes)

_____ lb. 20-penny (d) galvanized box (or common)

_____ lb. 16d galvanized box (or common)

_____ lb. 12d galvanized box (or common)

BOLTS, SCREWS, FASTENERS

_____ pieces (pc.) ½-inch "redi-bolt" plated threaded rod

_____ pc. _____ inch plated threaded rod

_____ pc. ½-inch plated nuts

_____ pc. _____ inch plated nuts

_____ pc. _____ (diameter) x _____ (length) plated hex-head bolts

_____ pc. _____ x _____ plated hex-head bolts

_____ pc. _____ x _____ plated carriage bolts

_____ pc. _____ x _____ plated carriage bolts

_____ pc. ¼-inch U-bolts

_____ pc. _____ inch U-bolts

_____ pc. _____ inch plated common washers

_____ pc. _____ inch plated common washers

_____ pc. _____ inch plated hex-head lag screws

_____ pc. _____ inch plated hex-head lag screws

_____ 2x6 universal hangers

_____ 2x2x3 galvanized sheet steel right angles

_____ pc. 1¼-inch galvanized right angles

_____ lb. _____ inch malleable flanges (washers)

_____ ft. plated ¼-inch chain

_____ pc. ¼-inch lap links

_____ pc. ⅜-inch eye bolts

MISCELLANEOUS ITEMS

_____ ft. ⅜-inch rope (Manila or nylon)

_____ ft. _____ inch rope

_____ sacks (90 lb.) ready-to-mix concrete

_____ pc. 21-foot-long, 1¼-inch-diameter galvanized pipe

_____ pc. _____ inch-long, 1¼-inch galvanized pipe

_____ pc. galvanized sheet steel, 4 feet x 10 feet (18 to 22 gauge)

_____ pc. stainless sheet steel, 4 feet x 10 feet (16 to 20 gauge)

_____ cubic ft. Olympia or other high-grade, clean sand

_____ gal. creosote

_____ gal. boiled linseed oil

_____ gal. penetrating sealer

_____ gal. clear wood preservative

_____ gal. paint thinner

Running nut down threaded rod.

Most commonly damaged tool (broken hacksaw blades from careless use) and wasted material (threaded rod).

Building with Concrete

Filling burlap bags. Buy premixed concrete or use this formula dry: 5 parts sand and gravel to 1 part dry cement (one structure pictured here required 16 tons of sand and gravel and 30 sacks of cement). Experiment with mixtures to get the best one for your structure. One cubic yard of this material weighs about 1 1/2 tons and will make a wall 1 foot thick, 3 feet high, and 9 feet long.

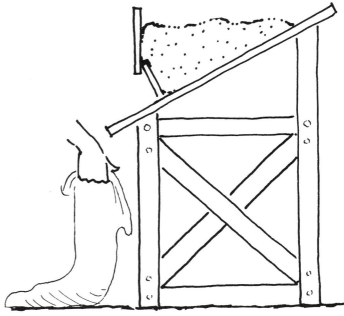

A slide chute helps load the heavy concrete.

Dry sacks forming arch.

Wet sacks in place.

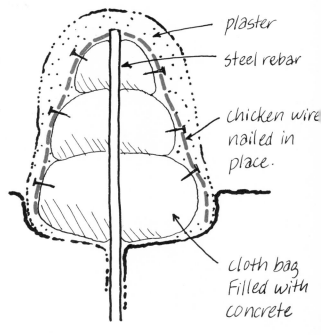

plaster

steel rebar

chicken wire nailed in place.

cloth bag filled with concrete

Mortar being applied over wet sacks. Note reinforcing steel and chicken wire. The mortar mixture is 4 shovels of Olympia sand to 1 shovel of dry cement and 1 part fire clay for every 10 parts of mortar mix. Vertical or overhanging parts of the structure are difficult to cover with mortar; to avoid problems, tie chicken wire onto these places and apply a coating of white glue to them before applying mortar. White glue also makes good joints between new work and dry areas. Frequent watering while the structure is drying will reduce cracks in the surface. The day's mortaring work will be hard the next morning but should be kept damp (by watering) for several days.

Troweling the surface smooth.

Kids leaving their mark.

A concrete dragon.

Ferroconcrete cave. Materials needed to build the structure pictured here include: 3 cubic yards of Olympia sand; 4 sacks of cement; 1 sack of Pozzolan (a fine-grained material); 15 pieces of 3/8 rebar steel, 20 feet long each; 40 pieces of 1/4 rebar steel, 20 feet long each; mild steel wire; and 6 1/2-inch-mesh, 22-gauge rolls of aviary netting. The basic shape is made of mild steel wire, in a grid of wires 6 inches apart; this shape is covered with aviary netting—four layers on top and two underneath the grid supply sufficient strength for a play sculpture. The aviary netting is stitched tightly to the structure with wire (stitches about 3 inches apart), a tedious but necessary procedure. Then the concrete is mixed (by combining sand, cement, Pozzolan, and water) and applied to the framework; the concrete should be worked thoroughly into the netting so that it is in contact with the metal at all points—this is how the structure gets its strength. The concrete must be applied to both sides of the framework to achieve this strength. Application of cement epoxy will make smooth sliding areas on the structure, and a disc sander can be used to remove rough edges.

Nobody's Perfect

A mistake industriously corrected; the post was cut too short, then patched with an extra piece to extend it to safety-rail height.

Mortar covering over stack sacks was too skimpy; this can be repaired by adequate replastering.

Example of a structure built by a community and an inexperienced designer. This playground illustrates three common pitfalls: (1) improper scale for kids; (2) inadequate provision for traffic flow between first and second platforms; and (3) dead-end top level, reached by a single ladder.

Example of a playground built with no design advice. Problems: no consideration given to movement of children through the space; and lack of play opportunities— what can kids do on that tree? The tower cage is a perfect site for king-of-the-mountain hassles.

8 Okay, Now What?

The preceding chapters have concentrated on how and why to build a playground, with particular emphasis on active-play structures. But children's environments can be enhanced in many other ways as well. Some specific examples follow, along with suggestions for providing play experiences for children with certain special needs.

"Special" Children Are Not Different

People tend to think that children with problems need a whole environment that is specially adapted for them. This is not the case, however; "special" children can adequately cope with most situations in everyday life. These children are not really different from others, whether their problem is physical, mental, or emotional—typically they are late in developing or learning some part of normal behavior.

Kids at play exhibit two kinds of judgment. The first is the innate instinct for self-preservation common to all persons; even a severely retarded child, for instance, won't walk off a cliff. The second type of judgment is based on learning, and this cognitive process is the one that develops much more slowly or not at all in some children. The actions of a retarded child on a play structure illustrate how innate judgment functions even if cognitive judgment is impaired. Such a child will come to the safety rail at the edge of a platform, for example, and carefully step over it, holding on all the while. He hadn't recognized the railing's purpose, but once on the outside of it he will instinctively hold on and try to find another foothold. His poorly developed cognitive judgment may prevent the child from retracing his steps, but his instinct for self-preservation will keep him holding on as long as he can. The danger is that such a child may tire and let go before anyone can help him get back over the railing.

Situations such as this can be avoided in environments for children whose cognitive development is impaired. Most of the design criteria and play experiences discussed in the foregoing chapters may be used in such playgrounds, with three additional considerations.

First, any play environment should provide for adequate flow of traffic at all points. Every area of the playground should have safe and easily seen exits, and all activities in the space should be obviously reversible. For example, a child may have little trouble climbing up a rope, but she might not know how to get down once she's at the top; and even if she knows what to do, the more difficult downward climb may be beyond her physical capacity. Consequently, such deceptively simple activities should be avoided.

Second, equipment should be selected very carefully for such environments. Since most of these children are developmentally out of step with others in their age group, they may need to work up to some of the activities commonly found in a playground. For instance, a child may be afraid to go into a tunnel because he can't perceive that it is big enough for his body, even though the tunnel has plenty of room for him. One way to help children overcome such a fear and improve their perception is to provide equipment that develops this skill in stages. The playground might include several tunnels; one would be a large, open tunnel with only floor and ceiling, another would be smaller but still open sided, and a third would be a conventional closed tunnel.

Finally, some children will have specific needs that are related to their problems, and these considerations will influence the design of a play environment. A space for kids with hearing loss must be arranged so that a teacher or other adult has ready access to them, since someone must touch a child to get his attention. For some children, alternative pathways may have to be developed for them to learn certain skills. A child may never perfect her balance on a balance beam, for example, but she might develop a sense of balance through swimming, since this

exercise could strengthen muscles that had previously been too weak to support her.

Projects Related to Playground Creation

ART PROJECTS   Many kinds of art projects could be correlated with playground building, and they offer another good source of involvement in the school for parents and community artists. Such an art program was founded five years ago in San Francisco by sculptor Ruth Asawa. This program has brought professional artists together with students, teachers, and parent volunteers in a number of public schools, where the projects have included mural painting, crafts, music, drama, and photography. In addition to offering new skills to students and parents and enriching the environments of many schools, this program provided the impetus for a citywide student art festival in the Civic Center plaza.

Another result of the school art program in San Francisco is an excellent book, *The Alvarado School-Community Art Program* (named for the first school to participate) by Joan Abrahamson and Sally Woodbridge. Besides documenting the experience of seven schools in the program, the book contains a detailed manual of instructions and suggestions for specific materials and projects, such as baker's clay (which is similar to modeling clay but can be fired in a conventional oven as well as in a kiln), kites, printmaking, tie-dyeing, and sewing. This very useful book can be ordered from the Alvarado Art Workshop,

Inc., c/o Art Department, San Francisco Unified School District, 135 Van Ness Avenue, San Francisco, Ca. 94102. The price is $3.00, postpaid.

FILM WORKSHOP Establishment of a children's film workshop in conjunction with playground creation offers a good means of documenting the whole process. One San Francisco filmmaker, Ben Spicer, started such a workshop by taking his two sons, age nine and ten, with him when he went to film a playground-construction day. Before long the boys were begging to use the Super 8-mm. camera and tape recorder, and the next weekend they brought some friends along to share in the filmmaking duties. Spicer also works as community liaison for several public schools, and recently his film workshops have become part of the regular activity for many elementary school children. Among the projects he hopes to complete this year will be a student-made film that depicts the variety of environments for children in the city, from barren, empty schoolyards to kid-built play structures. Persons interested in learning more about these workshops may write to Ben Spicer at 3461 16th Street, San Francisco, Ca. 94114.

DRAMA The platforms and equipment of a play structure can make a versatile and uncommon environment for plays, as well as for playing. In fact, drama instructor and director Geri Silk has founded a group called Theatre-Go-Round, which presents dramas on the playgrounds at schools in the San Francisco area. Geri fosters a spontaneous, playlike approach to acting, and she often takes her college classes to a community-built play structure for improvisational workshops. Last year the drama group adapted *Tom Sawyer* for presentation on the Theatre-Go-Round circuit of schools and community theaters, and Geri plans to add several more plays to the group's repertory this year. For a copy of her "How to Make a Play" (50¢), write Geri Silk at 3030 California Street, San Francisco, Ca. 94115.

GARDENS Even the most limited environment can have room for a garden if its planners use some imagination. One man with just such ingenuity is Tom Chiosso, a professional gardener for the San Francisco public schools. He has developed the "learning wall," a vertical framework that contains soil, plants, and panels for kids' artwork or curriculum materials. Chiosso emphasizes the value of children's planting a seed and then seeing the plant mature and bloom, as opposed to a two-week experiment that fizzles once the seeds have sprouted, which is what usually happens in the classroom.

The learning wall can also be a significant part of a school's curriculum. Numerous academic subjects could be related to this structure, such as having kids use metric-system values for all calculations in the project or experimenting with light, shade, water, and fertilizer to determine their effects on plants. Or a class might learn about another culture by growing plants, such as herbs, that are native to a country and then

using them to prepare the traditional foods of that nation.

Persons interested in this concept may contact Tom Chiosso about the vertical garden (a patent application is on file related to the structure). Inquiries should be addressed to Atlas Frame Company, 3030 17th Street, San Francisco, Ca. 94110.

Organizing to "Green" the Schoolyards

Once a community group has completed a playground, its members often are eager to take on new and bigger projects. For some concerned parents and educators in San Francisco, the new project became a movement to improve the schoolyards of all of the city's public schools. This group, Volunteers to Beautify Our Schools, invited all public schools to join in a proposal for federal revenue-sharing funds to "green" the schoolyards. Sixteen schools followed through on the proposal, and in the past year the parents, kids, and teachers at these schools have built playgrounds, painted murals, and planted trees and gardens.

In addition to successfully steering their funding proposal through the city government channels, the volunteers have helped each participating school with the planning and paperwork necessary to get its schoolyard-improvement project under way. The group also has sponsored several workshops on schoolyard beautification, and group members have worked closely with school district officials and school board members to continue and expand this program.

For more information about the Volunteers to Beautify Our Schools, write Naoma Sparks, 464 Day St., San Francisco, Ca. 94131.

Play Isn't Necessarily Just for Kids

ADULT PLAY   Lots of people are doing research on children's play, but nobody has paid much attention to the fact that adults can play too. Nobody, that is, until play therapist Marion Saltman founded the Center for the Study of Play, which is devoted to helping grown-ups get in touch with the child in themselves. Marion and codirector R. Glenn ("Bernie") Bernardi hold workshops on the S.S. Vallejo, a large, weathered houseboat that is moored in Sausalito, a suburb of San Francisco. This marvelous environment has almost anything a person could want for play—a beautiful papier mâché horse (strong enough to hold an adult) suspended from a roof beam; a puppet theatre just waiting to be brought to life; and a room full of costumes for fantasies that dress up. The atmosphere of this place is relaxed and supportive, and there's nobody to stop you from doing exactly as you please.

One major objective of these adult workshops, Marion points out, is to foster a playful attitude in people, to encourage them to take life and themselves a little less seriously. Besides the benefits this loosening up will bring to an individual, it probably will make him or her easier to be around.

An excellent description of the center and interview with Marion Saltman is contained

in *Getting Clear: Body Work for Women* by Anne Kent Rush. As this book goes to press, Marion reports that she is publishing a book for children and adults, entitled *Magic Carpet Trip*, and that she has begun work on a compilation of her experience and research on play for adults. For more information about the center, write Center for the Study of Play, Box 654, Waldo Point, Sausalito, Ca. 94965.

ZOO PLAY Now that the kids and the grown-ups have a place to play, what about the animals in the zoo? One group in San Francisco has begun to solve that problem by building play structures in the animals' cages. The Volunteers of the Zoo, organized four years ago by Jay Beckwith, spend Sunday mornings at the zoo, observing animals to determine what type of play environment would be appropriate for them, doing research in the zoo library, and designing and building play environments. These are projects for which the zoo staff does not have time or resources, and the volunteers have enjoyed cooperation from zoo officials.

The addition of play structures to animals' cages has brought some notable results. At least four animal pairs have mated and had offspring since getting the play apparatus in their cages; none of these animals had mated successfully before they had a place to play. The volunteers also have prepared graphics exhibits that give zoo patrons some idea of animals' behavior in their natural habitats and in captivity. One display shows examples of primates' facial expressions and explains their meanings; this gives zoo visitors a rudimentary introduction to the monkeys' language.

LIST OF PLAYGROUNDS

The following playgrounds designed and built by communities working with Jay Beckwith are pictured in this book:

Duboce Park
Golden Gate Park
Precita Park   } Recreation and Park Department, City of San Francisco
San Francisco Zoo
Commodore Sloat School
McKinley School   } San Francisco Unified School District
West Portal School
Child Study Center, California State University, San Francisco
Lilliput Child Care Center, Associated Students of California State University, San Francisco
Gateway Montessori School, San Francisco
Golden West YMCA, San Francisco
Mission Co-op Nursery School/Centro Latino, San Francisco
San Francisco School/Montessori, San Francisco
Stone Valley School, Alamo, Ca.
Marin Country Day School, Corte Madera, Ca.
Marin Child Care Center, Marin City, Ca.
Alto Edna McGuire School, Mill Valley, Ca.
Pacifica Parent Co-op Nursery/Pomo Park, Pacifica, Ca.
Sanchez School, Pacifica, Ca.
Westview School, Pacifica, Ca.
Fremont School, Salinas, Ca.

ADDITIONAL LEARNING MATERIALS

People at Play, the nonprofit corporation organized by Jay Beckwith, offers several multimedia learning aids for use by community groups. These include slide presentations for preschool- and elementary-school-age children, films on community creation of environments for children, and filmstrips and cassette-tape recordings for children. Memberships in the organization are available and include a newsletter. For more information about these materials, write People at Play, P.O. Box 14173, San Francisco, Ca. 94114.

Bibliography

PLAY

Caplan, Frank and Theresa. *The Power of Play*. Garden City, New York: Anchor Books, 1974. Paperback, $3.95. Academic and readable; a comprehensive overview of play in the whole fabric of life, with emphasis on play in childhood. Good bibliography.

Cass, Joan E. *Helping Children Grow Through Play*. New York: Schocken Books Inc., 1973. Experiential, personal account that includes comments from teachers and children; strong on child observation.

Herron, R. E., and Sutton-Smith, B. (eds.). *Child's Play*. New York: John Wiley & Sons, Inc., 1971. Compilation of basically scientific studies from several different approaches, including developmental, cognitive, and ecological. An especially interesting dialogue between the noted theorists Jean Piaget and Brian Sutton-Smith.

Huizinga, Johan. *Homo Ludens*. Boston: Beacon Press, 1955 (original edition, 1938). Paperback, $2.95. The first comprehensive statement on the cultural value of play. Excellent chapter on the significance of play to all societies.

Lowenfeld, Margaret. *Play in Childhood*. New York: John Wiley & Sons, Inc., 1967. Paperback, $2.25. Describes observation techniques, with analysis of many examples.

Millar, Susanna. *The Psychology of Play*. Baltimore: Penguin Books Inc., 1968. Paperback, $1.45. A compilation of European and American literature on psychology relating to play through 1968; extensive bibliography.

Piers, Maria W. (ed.). *Play and Development*. New York: W. W. Norton & Company, Inc., 1972. Transcript of a symposium with Piaget, Erikson, Lorenz, and other theorists. Good introduction to these important (and often difficult-to-read) thinkers.

Rush, Anne Kent. *Getting Clear: Body Work for Women*. New York: Random House/Bookworks, 1973. Paperback, $4.95. Contains a fifteen-page interview with Marion Saltman of the Center for the Study of Play.

PLAYGROUNDS

Aaron, David, and Winawer, Bonnie P. *Child's Play*. New York: Harper and Row, Publishers, 1965. An excellent critique of traditional play equipment and a clear, readable statement of the need for playgrounds.

Allen, Lady, of Hurtwood. *Planning for Play*. Cambridge, Mass.: The M.I.T. Press, 1968. Probably the most useful book on playgrounds; full of ideas, from adventure playgrounds to tailored, rather formal environments. A must for persons interested in adventure playgrounds.

Bengtsson, Arvid (ed.). *Adventure Playgrounds*. New York: Praeger Publishers, Inc., 1972. $18.50. Experiential reporting on all European adventure playgrounds.

Cooper, Clare C. "Adventure Playgrounds." Reprint of article in *Landscape Architecture,* October, 1970. $1.00. (Available from Department of Landscape Architecture, 202 Wurster Hall, University of California, Berkeley, Ca. 94702.) Good introduction to adventure playgrounds; strong case for their use in the U.S.

Dattner, R. *Design for Play*. New York: Van Nostrand Reinhold Company, 1969. The best overview available of playground possibilities; many good illustrations.

D'Eugenio, Terry. *Building with Tires.* Cambridge, Mass.: Advisory for Open Education (90 Sherman St., Cambridge, Mass.), 1971. (Write for list of publications.) An inexpensive place to start.

Farallones Scrapbook. Farallones Institute, 1971. Paperback, $4.50. (Available from Farallones Designs, Star Route, Pt. Reyes Station, Ca. 94956.) Strong on the casual approach to changing classrooms and building playgrounds.

Friedberg, P. M., and Berkeley, E. P. *Play and Interplay.* New York: Macmillan Publishing Co., Inc., 1970. $9.95. An architect looks at the city and play; interesting if you want to put a park around a skyscraper. Of some value for students of inner-city life.

Helick, R. M., and Watkins, M. T. *The Playyard at Louise.* Pittsburgh: Regent Graphic Services, 1973. Paperback, $16.00. An architect's research on what a playground should include; a somewhat superficial compilation of answers to a nationwide survey. Expensive for the amount of useful information.

Lederman, A., and Trachsel, A. *Creative Playground and Recreation Centers.* New York: Praeger Publishers, Inc., 1968. A survey of playgrounds; some good photos.

Moore, Robin C. *Open Space Learning Place.* 1973. $1.00. (Available from Department of Landscape Architecture, 202 Wurster Hall, University of California, Berkeley, Ca. 94702.)

————. *Washington Environmental Yard.* $1.00. (Available from above address.)

————, Ford, Patsy, and Malcolm, Carol. *Living Kid City.* 1973. $2.00. (Available from above address.) All of these books are filled with ideas; particularly strong on curriculum uses of the play environment.

Osmon, F. L. *Patterns for Designing Children's Centers.* New York: Educational Facilities Laboratories (477 Madison Avenue, N.Y. 10022), 1971. (Write for list of publications.) Gives excellent conceptual and design tools for making changes in environments for preschool centers.

Sharkey, Tony. *Building a Playground.* Educational Development Center (55 Chapel St., Newton, Mass.

02160), 1970. (Write for list of publications.) The story of a Head Start Program whose participants built their own playground.

Stone, J., and Rudolph, N. *Play and Playgrounds.* National Association for the Education of Young Children (1834 Connecticut Ave., N.W., Washington, D.C. 20009), 1970. (Write for list of publications.) Picture book of playgrounds; short on information.

DESIGN

Ardalan, N., and Bakhtiar, L. *The Sense of Unity: The Sufi Tradition in Persian Architecture.* Bridge between design and mysticism; considers spiritual growth in the context of environmental forms.

Fuller, R. Buckminster. *Earth, Inc.* Garden City, New York: Anchor Books, 1973. Paperback, $2.95. A door to the future.

————. *No More Secondhand God and Other Writings.* Carbondale: Southern Illinois University Press, 1963. Paperback, $2.45. Contains "Universal Requirements of a Dwelling Advantage," which is an impeccable list of steps by which one discovers a truly unique design. Demanding reading, but a tool for achieving clear thinking.

Holden, Alan. *Shapes, Space, and Symmetry.* New York: Columbia University Press, 1971. $5.95. One of the best of many books to help you find your way through shapes other than the square. Profusely illustrated.

Kahn, Lloyd. *Shelter.* Bolinas, Ca., Shelter Publications (P. O. Box 279, Bolinas, Ca. 94924), 1973. Paperback, $6.00. Houses can be playgrounds too. Another big-format book to turn you on to the potential of living in harmony with your environment.

————. *Dome Book II.* Bolinas, Ca., Shelter Publications (P. O. Box 279, Bolinas, Ca. 94924), 1971. Paperback, $4.00. If you want to build a dome, get this book.

Sanoff, H. *Learning Environments for Children.* Raleigh: School of Design, North Carolina State University, 1972. $3.00. Good for changing indoor spaces.

Woodbridge, Sally. *Ruth Asawa's San Francisco Fountain.* Published by the author, 1973. (Available from the bookstore at the San Francisco Museum of

Art, Van Ness and McAllister, San Francisco, Ca. 94102.) $1.50. Story of the creation of a fountain in downtown San Francisco by sculptor Ruth Asawa, which was made from bronze-cast panels of baker's clay sculpture. Kids helped create the original panels.

EDUCATION—THEORY AND PRACTICE

Abrahamson, Joan, and Woodbridge, Sally. *The Alvarado School-Community Art Program.* 1973. (Available from Alvarado Art Workshop, c/o Art Department, San Francisco Unified School District, 135 Van Ness Avenue, San Francisco, Ca. 94102.) $3.00. Excellent documentation and manual for community-based art programs in public schools.

Fuller, R. Buckminster. *Education Automation.* Carbondale: Southern Illinois University Press, 1962. Paperback, $1.95. Fuller's statement on education.

———. *Ideas and Integrities.* Toronto: Macmillan Publishing Co., Inc., 1969. Paperback, $1.95. Autobiographical; how Fuller's childhood experiences formed the basis of his personality.

Greer, Colin (ed.). *The Solution as Part of the Problem.* New York: Perennial Library, 1973. Paperback, $1.25. Evaluates the consequences of deschooling and community control of schools.

Gross, P., and Railton, E. *Teaching Science in an Outdoor Environment.* Berkeley: University of California Press, 1972. $2.95. A place to start the greening of your schoolyard.

Hainstock, Elizabeth G. *Teaching Montessori in the Home.* New York: Random House, Inc., 1968. The simplest statement of the Montessori method.

Leonard, George. *Education and Ecstasy.* New York: Delacorte Press, 1968. Overview of the future possibilities for education; see especially "Visiting Day, 2001 A.D.," a vision of the ideal school.

Montessori, Maria. *Spontaneous Activity in Education.* New York: Schocken Books Inc., 1965. Paperback, $2.95. The basic Montessori text.

Piaget, Jean. *Play, Dreams, and Imitation in Childhood.* New York: W. W. Norton & Company, Inc., 1962. Paperback, $2.95. The most relevant to play theory of the many Piaget writings.

Shah, Idries. *The Pleasantries of the Incredible Mulla Nasrudin.* New York: E. P. Dutton & Co., Inc., 1971. Paperback, $1.75. Education through laughter and storytelling.

Sharkey, Tony. *Cardboard Carpentry Workshop.* Newton, Mass.: Educational Development Center (55 Chapel St., Newton, Mass. 02160), 1968. (Write for list of publications.) Picture-story of designing and building with cardboard.

PSYCHOLOGY

Erikson, Erik. *Childhood and Society.* New York: W. W. Norton & Company, Inc., 1950. Foundation for modern child psychology.

Moustakas, Clark (ed.). *The Child's Discovery of Himself.* New York: Ballantine Books, Inc., 1969. Paperback, $1.25. An introduction to existential psychology with children.

Ornstein, Robert E. *The Psychology of Consciousness.* San Francisco: W. H. Freeman & Company, 1972. Paperback, $3.50. Fascinating, readable foray into the world of perception, cognition, and consciousness.

Rogers, Carl. *On Becoming a Person.* Boston: Houghton Mifflin Company, 1970. Paperback, $3.25. After you've dug a hole with the Freudians, use Rogers to get yourself out.

Sutton-Smith, Brian. *The Developmental Psychology of Children's Games.* Baltimore: Penguin Books Inc., 1973. Latest book by a leader in child theory.

BEHAVIOR

Birdwhistell, Ray. *Kinesics and Context.* New York: Ballantine Books, Inc., 1972. Paperback, $1.95. Basic text in body language.

Eibl-Eibesfeldt, I. *Ethology: The Biology of Behavior.* New York: Holt, Rinehart and Winston, Inc., 1970. A thorough, readable, and well-illustrated introduction to this new and fascinating field of science.

Goffman, Erving. *Interaction Ritual.* Garden City, N.Y.: Anchor Books, 1967. Paperback, $1.95.

———. *The Presentation of Self in Everyday Life.* Garden City, N.Y.: Anchor Books, 1959. Paperback, $1.25. Companion pieces on the sociology of relationships. A compelling argument for socially supportive environments for young children.

Hall, Edward. *The Hidden Dimension*. New York: Doubleday & Company, Inc., 1969. Basic text on the anthropology of environments.

Isaacs, Susan. *Social Development in Young Children*. New York: Schocken Books Inc., 1972. New work by a major theorist in the field of child studies.

Lorenz, Konrad. *On Aggression*. New York: Bantam Books, Inc., 1970. Paperback, $1.45. Most available book by the major ethologist; illustrates territoriality in human behavior.

Morris, Desmond (ed.). *Primate Ethology*. Garden City, N.Y.: Anchor Books, 1969. Paperback, $2.45. A collection of articles by major ethologists, including an ethological study of children in nursery schools.

THE BODY—PHILOSOPHY AND SKILLS

Ayres, A. Jean. *Sensory Integration and Learning Disorders*. Los Angeles: Western Psychological Services, 1972. The best book available on body skills, as told by an eminent physical therapist; scholarly, with an excellent bibliography.

Cratty, Bryant J. *Teaching Motor Skills*. Englewood Cliffs, N.J.: Prentice-Hall, Inc., 1973. Paperback, $4.50. The physical education approach at its best.

Feldenkrais, Moshe. *Awareness Through Movement*. New York: Harper & Row, Publishers, 1972. $5.95. Attempts to create a graceful, fluid body through expansion of awareness and relaxation, as opposed to the vigorous calisthenic approach.

Ferretti, Fred. *The Great American Marble Book*. New York: Workman Publishing Co., Inc., 1973. Paperback, $2.50. A book about muscle skills that children will enjoy.

Frostig, M., and Maslow, P. *Movement Education: Theory and Practice*. Chicago: Follett Publishing Co., 1970. $8.00. (Also available: *Frostig Move-Grow-Learn Program*, 181 Exercise Cards and Teacher's Guide; $14.00.) Very thorough program of perceptual-motor-development skills for children.

Hanna, Thomas. *Bodies in Revolt*. New York: Delta Books, 1970. Paperback, $2.65. Looks at major thinkers of the 19th and 20th centuries from the viewpoint of the total person—the body is not separate from the brain. Discusses work of Piaget, Camus, Kant, Darwin, Nietzsche, and others.

Opie, Iona and Peter. *Children's Games in the Street and Playground*. London: Oxford University Press, 1969. Thorough treatment of children's games.

Acknowledgments

The preparation of this book was made easier by the help and encouragement of many friends. I especially wish to thank David Gast for his help in preparing the checklists and the use of his polyhedron hill design; the members of Volunteers to Beautify Our Schools, particularly Ynez Flo, Ruthann Lehrer, and Elena Perkins, whose interest was a source of energy for me (besides which, they fed me quite often); Carolyn Weil, who added a refreshing perspective to the whole process; Ben Spicer, whose films and photos helped capture the spirit of community involvement; Paul Crowley, Bob Berke, and Bill Hayward, for their slide show and soundtrack; Chong Lee, for his excellent and prompt printing of photographs; and the staff of People at Play, who learned as I did and asked many questions that helped me get this information down on paper.

Index